LIVING THE

RESURRECTION

LIVING THE

RESURRECTION

THE
RISEN
CHRIST
in
Everyday
Life

EUGENE H.
PETERSON

NAVPRESS®

BRINGING TRUTH TO LIFE

OUR GUARANTEE TO YOU

The Navigators is an international Christian organization. Our mission is to reach, disciple, and equip people to know Christ and to make Him known through successive generations. We envision multitudes of diverse people in the United States and every other nation who have a passionate love for Christ, live a lifestyle of sharing Christ's love, and multiply spiritual laborers among those without Christ.

NavPress is the publishing ministry of The Navigators. NavPress publications help believers learn biblical truth and apply what they learn to their lives and ministries. Our mission is to stimulate spiritual formation among our readers.

ISBN 1-57683-929-X

Cover design by The DesignWorks Group, Inc. / John Hamilton, www.thedesignworksgroup.com
Cover photo by Images.com
Creative Team: Terry Behimer, Don Simpson, Arvid Wallen, Kathy Mosier, Rose Yancik

Some of the anecdotal illustrations in this book are true to life and are included with the permission of the persons involved. All other illustrations are composites of real situations, and any resemblance to people living or dead is coincidental.

The text of this book is adapted from three lectures given by Eugene H. Peterson on May 18–19, 2001, at Regent College, Vancouver, British Columbia.

Some of the material in this book will appear in a forthcoming volume by Eugene H. Peterson titled *Practice Resurrection* and is used here by permission of Wm. B. Eerdmans Publishing Company.

Unless otherwise identified, all Scripture quotations in this publication are taken from the *Revised Standard Version Bible* (RSV), copyright 1946, 1952, 1971, by the Division of Christian Education of the National Council of the Churches of Christ in the USA, used by permission. Other versions used include: the HOLY BIBLE: NEW INTERNATIONAL VERSION® (NIV®), Copyright © 1973, 1978, 1984 by International Bible Society, used by permission of Zondervan Publishing House, all rights reserved; *THE MESSAGE* (MSG). Copyright © 1993, 1994, 1995, 1996, 2000, 2001, 2002. Used by permission of NavPress Publishing Group; the *New Revised Standard Version* (NRSV), copyright © 1989, by the Division of Christian Education of the National Council of the Churches of Christ in the USA, used by permission, all rights reserved; and the *King James Version* (KJV).

Peterson, Eugene H., 1932-
   Living the Resurrection : the risen Christ in everyday life / Eugene H. Peterson.
      p. cm.
   Includes bibliographical references.
   ISBN 1-57683-929-X
   1. Jesus Christ—Resurrection—Biblical teaching. 2. Christian life
3. Bible. N.T. Gospels—Criticism, interpretation, etc. I. Title.
   BT482.P48 2006
   248.4--dc22
                              2005022948

Published in association with the literary agency of Alive Communications, Inc., 7680 Goddard Street, Suite 200, Colorado Springs, CO 80920 (www.alivecommunications.com).

Printed in the United States of America

1 2 3 4 5 6 / 10 09 08 07 06

FOR A FREE CATALOG OF
NAVPRESS BOOKS & BIBLE STUDIES,
CALL 1-800-366-7788 (USA)
OR 1-800-839-4769 (CANADA)

CONTENTS

The women, deep in wonder and full of joy, lost no time in leaving the tomb. They ran to tell the disciples. Then Jesus met them, stopping them in their tracks. "Good morning!" he said. They fell to their knees, embraced his feet, and worshiped him. (MATTHEW 28:8-9, MSG)

CHAPTER ONE

Resurrection Wonder

I've always liked Billy Sunday's formula for the ideal
Christian life. Billy Sunday was the quintessential
American mass evangelist. He crisscrossed North America
one hundred years ago with his flamboyant revival show-
manship, which attracted enormous crowds. He was an
ex–baseball player, and he used his pulpit as a pitcher's
mound, winding up and letting go of his fastball, screw-
ball, knuckleball sermons night after night in his huge
revival tents. One of the features of these tents was the
sawdust trail. The wide aisle leading from the entrance of
the tent down to the elevated pulpit from which Sunday
preached was layered with a couple of inches of sawdust.
It kept down the dust in dry times and moderated the
mud in wet times. But it also marked the trail from row
after row of folding chairs to the altar at the front of the
tent, just below the pulpit. As Billy Sunday would wind
up his sermon, he would give his famous "altar call," calling
men and women who had come to the tent that night to
step out of their seats, walk down the sawdust trail to the

altar, and, kneeling there, become Christians. "Hitting the sawdust trail" entered the North American vocabulary as a synonym for repentance and conversion.

The Perfect Formula

I don't know if "hitting the sawdust trail" was coined by Billy Sunday, but he was most certainly the one who gave it currency as a stock phrase in our language. His often-repeated formula for the ideal Christian life was this: "Hit the sawdust trail, fall on your knees, and receive Christ as your Savior. Then walk out of this tent into the street, get hit by a Mack truck, and go straight to heaven."

You must admit, I think, that it's a wonderful formula for getting to heaven the quickest and easiest way. And virtually foolproof. There is no time to backslide, no temptations to bother with, no doubts to wrestle with, no spouse to have to honor, no kids to put up with, no enemies to love, no more sorrow, no more tears. Instant eternity.

Billy Sunday is an extreme case of what is more or less typical of the North American approach to these matters: Get it right, but then get it done as quickly as possible. Define your goal and then go for it, devising the most economical and efficient means. As a culture, we are great at beginnings. We set magnificent goals. But in the in-between, we don't have much to write home about. When things get bad enough, we just make a new beginning, which we are very good at doing. Or we set a new goal or "vision" or "mission statement," as we call it, which temporarily distracts us from what is going on right around us.

WHAT THE CHURCH LEAVES OUT

Let me paraphrase something that Pope John Paul II once said as he addressed a group of leaders from Third World countries: Don't look at the Western nations for models in your development. They know how to make things, but they don't know how to live with them. They have acquired a mind-boggling technology, but they've forgotten how to raise their children.

This is the context for this book. It's a cultural context in which souls are pretty much ignored in the rush of getting something or making something. The formation of souls is a major responsibility of the Christian church— lives formed by the Holy Spirit "to the measure of the stature of the fulness of Christ" (Ephesians 4:13). But by and large, it is a neglected responsibility. We have a lot of special programs to take care of it, but they are always at the periphery of something else. There is far more attention being given to spiritual formation in the secular world of New Age spirituality and psychological development than in the church. And however laudable the attention being given by the teachers and guides of this world, they are attempting to do it quite apart from Jesus Christ or with Jesus only at the margins. Therefore, they are leaving out the biggest part, which is resurrection.

My conviction is that the church is the community that God has set at the center of the world to keep the world centered. One essential aspect of this centering is commonly called spiritual formation—the lifelong formation of the life of Christ in us. It consists of what goes on between the moment we realize and accept our identity as Christians and the time when we sit down to "the marriage supper of the Lamb" (Revelation 19:9). It deals with the way we live in the time being, the time that intervenes between kneeling at the altar and getting hit by the Mack truck.

I take up this subject with considerable urgency, not only because of the widespread secularization of spiritual formation in the culture around us, but also because the church in which I live and have been called to write and speak has become more like the culture in these matters than counter to it. The enormous interest in "spirituality" these days is not accompanied by much, if any, interest in the long and intricate and daily business of formation in Christ—that is, the practice of the dispositions and habits of the heart that changes our word *spirituality* from a wish or a desire or a fantasy or a diversion into an actual life lived to the glory of God. A phrase from a Wendell Berry poem gives focus to what we're doing—"practice resurrection." I'm going to anchor this book in the resurrection of Jesus.

RECOVERING OUR RESURRECTION CENTER

We live the Christian life out of a rich tradition of formation-by-resurrection. Jesus' resurrection provides the energy and conditions by which we "walk before the LORD in the land of the living"—the great psalm phrase (116:9). The resurrection of Jesus creates and then makes available the reality in which we are formed as new creatures in Christ by the Holy Spirit. The do-it-yourself, self-help culture of North America has so thoroughly permeated our imaginations that we ordinarily don't give attention to the biggest thing of all—resurrection. And the reason we don't is because resurrection is not something we can use or control or manipulate or improve on. It's interesting, isn't it, that the world has had very little success in commercializing Easter—turning it into a commodity—as it has

Christmas? If we can't, in our phrase, "get a handle on it" or use it, we soon lose interest. But resurrection is not available for our use. It's exclusively God's operation.

What I want to do is recover our resurrection center and embrace the formation traditions that develop out of it. I'm going to deal in turn with three aspects of Jesus' resurrection that define and energize us as we enter the practice of resurrection lives. I will then set this resurrection life lived out of the reality and conditions of Jesus' resurrection in contrast to what I consider the common cultural habits and assumptions that are either oblivious to or make detours around resurrection. I will name this "the deconstruction of resurrection." Finally, I will suggest something of what is involved in cultivating the practice of resurrection: living appropriately and responsively in a world in which Christ is risen.

Reverence and Intimacy Need Each Other

Our four Gospel writers all complete their narrations of the gospel of Jesus with a story or stories of Jesus' resurrection. They come at it from different directions and provide different details, but one element is common to each of them: a sense of wonder, astonishment, surprise. Despite the several hints scattered throughout the Hebrew

Scriptures and Jesus' three explicit statements forecasting his resurrection (see Mark 8:31; 9:31; 10:34), when it happened, it turned out that no one—no one—expected it. The first people involved in Jesus' resurrection were totally involved in dealing with his death. Now they had to do a complete about-face and deal with a life. As they did it, they were suffused with wonder.

Matthew gives us Mary Magdalene and a woman he names "the other Mary" making an early Sunday morning visit to the tomb in which on late Friday afternoon they had watched Joseph of Arimathea place Jesus' crucified body (see 28:1-10). As they approach the tomb, the ground suddenly shakes under their feet—an earthquake. This is followed by a blaze of lightning, which turns out to be an angel. The combination of earthquake and lightning puts the Roman soldiers who are guarding this tomb out of commission. Scared out of their wits, they sprawl on the ground in a dead faint.

But the two Marys stay on their feet and hear the angel address them personally with two phrases: "Do not be afraid" and "He has risen" (verses 5-6). The angel then gives them a message to be delivered to the disciples. They leave the site of the tomb, as ordered by the angel. Deep in wonder and full of joy, they are off on the run to share the news with the disciples. But then they are stopped in their tracks by a greeting: "Good morning!" (verse 9, MSG). They hear a welcome in the greeting and fall to their knees before the resurrected Jesus. Their first response to the risen Christ was to kneel in awed reverence. There was also an element of intimacy in that reverence, for they dared to touch and hold on to his feet: They "worshiped him" (verse 9).

The two elements together became worship. Falling to our knees before Jesus—an act of reverence—is not in itself resurrection worship. Touching and holding the feet of Jesus—an act of intimacy—is not in itself resurrection worship. The acts of reverence and intimacy need each other. The reverence needs the infusion of intimacy lest it become a cool and detached aesthetic. The intimacy needs to be suffused in reverence lest it become a gushy emotion. These women knew what they were doing: They were dealing with God in the living presence of Jesus, and so they worshiped.

Jesus then repeats the angel's earlier reassurance—"Do not be afraid"—and repeats the message to be delivered to the disciples. And that was it.

I love the contrast between those Roman guards—insensible and sprawled on the ground, paralyzed by fear—and the two exuberant women kneeling on the same ground, energized by fear. It's the same word in both cases—*fear*. But it's not the same thing. There is a fear that incapacitates us for dealing with God, and there is a fear that pulls us out of our preoccupation with ourselves, our feelings, or our circumstances into a world of wonder. It pulls us out of ourselves into the very action of God.

SHATTERING ASTONISHMENT

Mark adds another woman—Salome—to Matthew's two Marys on their early Sunday morning visit to the tomb, and then he adds some details that reinforce the sense of resurrection wonder (see 16:1-8). Mark tells us that the three women are coming to the tomb prepared to do a job— embalm Jesus' body with spices. As they approach, they are preoccupied with a problem: How are they going to get into the tomb and do their work? A huge stone had been rolled in front of the entrance, and they would never be able to move it. But when they arrive, they find that the stone has been rolled back. Big surprise! They expected to have to deal with a big problem, but there is no problem. They expected to do an important and essential job, but there is no job to do.

Their surprise is compounded when they enter the tomb and find a young man—we assume it was an angel—sitting there ready to talk with them. These women are "completely taken aback, astonished" (verse 5, MSG). Who wouldn't be? But he reassures them. He tells them that Jesus has been raised and gives them the message to deliver to the disciples.

Mark, in his terse, abrupt ending, highlights the shattering astonishment experienced by these three women. The women were "beside themselves, their heads swimming." They were "stunned" and "said nothing to anyone" (verse 8, MSG). Resurrection wonder, indeed.

Remembering Jesus' Words

Luke includes a number of unnamed women with the two Marys and Salome in this opening resurrection scene (see 24:1-12). These unnamed women are "the women who had come with him [Jesus] from Galilee" (23:55). They are also referred to as "the women" (24:1, MSG) and "the other women" (verse 10). He also adds a fourth named woman, Joanna (see verse 10). They show up with their burial spices, intending to go to work on Jesus' body. But, of course, there is no body. They are "puzzled" (verse 4, MSG). They scratch their heads and look around. This is the right tomb, isn't it? On Friday afternoon they had been right there watching Joseph of Arimathea place Jesus' body in it. They had spent Saturday getting the burial spices and ointments together. By now, they have spent hours in preparation getting ready for this devout act of loving service to this person who had meant so much to them and whom they are now mourning. And now this. *What's going on here, anyway?*

Then, suddenly, two men are right there before them. Clean light cascades through and off their clothes. They have got to be angels. Totally frightened, the women fall down—their faces to the ground. The two men in the tomb reassure them by saying, "Why are you looking for the Living One in a cemetery? He is not here, but raised up. Remember how he told you when you were still back in Galilee that he had to be handed over to sinners, be killed on a cross, and in three days rise up?" (verses 5-7, MSG).

Well, these women do remember. They had heard those words. But never in their wildest dreams had they expected it—not in their lifetimes. They are understandably disoriented. But the two men's matter-of-fact words reconnect them with matter-of-fact reality. They remember where they had been—those very real Galilean roads and meals and conversations. They remember what they have just lived through—an excruciating Jerusalem crucifixion. They remember Jesus' words—words they had heard with their own ears. How could they forget them?

The women remember. No, they are not crazy. Soon they have their feet under them again and go back and tell the disciples. They have no luck getting the disciples in on what they now know and experience. The disciples dismiss their report as an idle tale. They don't believe a word of it. They think they are making it all up.

The Nature of Wonder

It's not easy to convey a sense of wonder, let alone resurrection wonder, to another. It's the very nature of wonder to catch us off guard, to circumvent expectations and assumptions. Wonder can't be packaged, and it can't be worked up. It requires some sense of being there and some sense of engagement.

Luke adds still another detail. He introduces the person of Peter as the first male to enter this scene of resurrection wonder. In the midst of the disciples' general disbelief that greets the women, Luke tells us that Peter jumps to his feet, runs to the tomb, stoops to look in, and sees a few grave clothes. That was all. He walks away puzzled, shaking his head. Obviously, we are not dealing with something that, as we say, "makes sense." Nor has anyone so far been able to "make something of it."

Two of our primary ways of dealing with reality are by understanding and by using. Understanding takes a new item of experience or information and makes sense of it by fitting it into all the other things we already know. Using tests out the new experience or information in the actual routines of what can be or has to be done. But this resurrection is inaccessible to either of these. Understanding and using are displaced by sheer wonder, astonishment, amazement—first by the women and then by Peter, who was just as stumped by what he was dealing with as were the women.

A Giveaway Detail

John, as is often his wont, does something quite different from his canonical brothers (see 20:1-19). He ratchets the sense of resurrection wonder up still another notch. John begins with Mary Magdalene arriving predawn on that Sunday morning at the tomb and then completely misinterpreting what she sees. She discovers that the tomb is empty and jumps to what would appear to be the obvious conclusion—robbery. Grave robbers. Grave robbery was a common and serious problem in those days, enough so as to provoke an imperial Roman edict against it.[1] Mary's sense of reality, it seems, was completely intact. She was quite able to look at evidence and come to a sober conclusion. Why else would the grave be empty?

Mary runs to tell Peter and "the other disciple"—we think it was John (verse 3). The two men immediately take off running to the tomb. They enter the tomb (Mary herself, it seems, hadn't gone in). They find that it is indeed empty, but they come to a completely different conclusion than Mary did. The conclusion they come to is resurrection.

And here's how they did it. John notices a striking and, as it turns out, giveaway detail. The kerchief that was used to cover Jesus' head was separate from the cloths that wrapped his body and was, in his phrase, "neatly folded by itself" (verse 7, MSG). John, with the quick mind of a born detective, deduces that robbery is out of the question. Grave robbers would not have unwrapped the corpse. And even if by some strange perversity they had, it is difficult to imagine them taking the time to neatly fold the head kerchief and set it aside. John—his mind working with surprising coolness under the emotion of the moment and on the strength of that single clue (the neatly folded kerchief)—comes up with what turns out to be the truth. Resurrection. And with that, John and Peter leave the tomb.

RABBONI!

The Gospel writer now returns the story to Mary. After delivering her message to the disciples—the message that fired the starting pistol that sent Peter and John running off on their resurrection-morning race—she comes back to the tomb, still operating under the misapprehension that Jesus' body was stolen. She is outside the tomb, distraught and heartbroken and weeping. When she kneels to look inside the tomb, she sees two angels. They ask sympathetically about her weeping. She tells them the reason and then turns away. Peripherally, she notices the figure of a man she doesn't recognize but assumes is the gardener. The man asks her the same question as the angels, and she gives the same answer. Then he speaks her name: "Mary" (verse 16).

She turns to face him, her tear-blurred eyes now clear. She sees Jesus, and she answers, "Rabboni!"—Teacher (verse 16). The term *Rabboni* combines the deep reverence for a person (rabbi) with an affectionate intimacy (probably something like "my dear Teacher").[2]

The fourth Gospel presents the opening scene of Jesus' resurrection somewhat differently from its predecessors but is no less charged with wonder. To Peter, who is mentioned briefly by Luke, another man is added to the scenario: "the disciple whom Jesus loved" (21:20)—the beloved disciple, whom we think was John. The two men get a story of their own. Their story is framed by Mary Magdalene first running from the tomb to sound the alarm and then returning to the tomb weeping, disconsolate in her loss. Her alarm kicked off the famous Peter-John race, which resulted in the first solid resurrection thinking. After the race, her tears lead us into the intimate resurrection recognition exchange: "Mary . . . Rabboni—my dear Teacher!"

We Can't Master Spiritual Formation

As we take in and meditate on the four resurrection accounts, our sense of resurrection wonder accumulates. It is a cumulative, building sense. These four stories are spare, compact, economically narrated. No purple passages in here. From this bedrock narrative austerity, though, a few things emerge with clarity, things that are significant as we ponder for ourselves formation-by-resurrection.

First, however many resurrection "hints and guesses" there may have been in the Hebrew, Mediterranean, and Near Eastern centuries preceding this, when it happened, it took those who were closest to the event and best prepared for it totally unawares. I think this is important. We're never in a position to know very much about formation-by-resurrection. This is not in continuity with or analogous to anything we're familiar with—psychological development, for instance, or moral metaphysics.

Second, it is obvious that no one did anything to prepare for what actually happened. There was no working-up readiness for it. The two Jewish religious groups who at the time were working most diligently to prepare the resurrection and Messianic ground for something just like this—the Pharisees and the Essenes—were looking the other way, and they missed it totally. Everyone is a beginner in this business. There are no experts.

Given the care that we, in our way of going about things, take to prepare, plan, and train for something that is big and important, that's more than a little disconcerting. Spiritual formation is not something we master. It's not something over which we have much, if any, control.

Third, marginal people in the culture —in this case, women—play a prominent role in perception and response. Although recognized leaders, such as Peter and John, aren't excluded, Mary Magdalene—perhaps the most marginal of any of the early followers of Jesus—is the chief resurrection witness and the only person to appear in all four accounts. The only fact that we know about Mary Magdalene before she joined Jesus is that she was possessed by "seven devils" and had been delivered from them. The "seven devils" could refer to an utterly dissolute moral life or to an extreme form of mental illness. Either or both of these pre-Jesus conditions, coupled with being a woman in a patriarchal society, put her at the very far edge of marginality.

Given the importance that we in our society give to celebrity endorsements, that's more than a little disconcerting. The men and women who are going to be most valuable to us in spiritual formation-by-resurrection are most likely going to be people at the edge of respectability: the poor, minorities, the suffering, the rejected, poets, and children.

Fourth, the resurrection was a quiet business that took place in a quiet place without publicity or spectators. There was, of course, much energy and emotion (tears, running, astonishment, bewilderment, and joy), but there was nothing to catch the attention of outsiders. (Matthew's earthquake is a partial exception to this. But the only outside people who were told or who were affected were the Roman guards who were knocked insensible by it.)

When I was young, I played a trumpet. In Montana where I grew up, Easter always took place just at the edge of winter. I was up at five, five thirty, or six every Easter morning for a sunrise service. Everybody wanted a trumpet player on Easter. My lips numb with cold on a frozen mouthpiece, I was there playing cracked notes on some hilltop around our town. But the point is that you make a lot of noise. This is important, and you let the whole world know it's important. Well, my church didn't get that from these Gospel texts.

Given our accustomed ways of surrounding the important events with attention-getting publicity and given the importance of this event for the gospel, that's a big surprise. Bright lights and amplification are not accessories to spiritual formation.

ENCOUNTERING THE "MORE AND OTHER"

And a fifth observation is fear. Fear is the most frequently mentioned resurrection response—six times in these four stories. We're afraid when we're suddenly caught off our guard and don't know what to do. We're afraid when our presuppositions and assumptions no longer account for what we're up against, and we don't know what will happen to us. We're afraid when reality, without warning, is shown to be either more or other than we thought it was.

But these six fear references take place in a tradition of

storytelling in the Hebrew culture and the Hebrew Scriptures in which the word *fear* is frequently used in a way that means far more than simply being scared. Here's the thing: It *includes* all the emotions that accompany being scared— disorientation, not knowing what's going to happen, the realization that there is far more here than we had any idea of. But that "more and other" is God.

Fear-of-the-Lord is the stock biblical term for this either sudden or cultivated awareness that the presence or revelation of God introduces into our lives. We are not the center of our existence. We are not the sum total of what matters. We don't know what's going to happen next.

Fear-of-the-Lord keeps us on our toes with our eyes open. Something is going on around here, and we don't want to miss it. Fear-of-the-Lord prevents us from thinking that we know it all. And it therefore prevents us from closing off our minds or our perceptions from what is new. Fear-of-the-Lord prevents us from acting presumptuously and therefore destroying or violating some aspect of beauty, truth, or goodness that we don't recognize or don't understand.

Fear-of-the-Lord is fear with the scary element deleted. So it is often accompanied with the reassurance: "Fear not." But the "fear not" does not result in the absence of fear but rather the transformation into fear-of-the-Lord.

We still don't know what's going on. We're still not in control. We're still deep, deep in mystery.

In the canonical resurrection stories, there are six occurrences of various forms of the root word *fear*. Twice the word is used to express terror: the Roman guards before the dazzling angel at the empty tomb (see Matthew 28:4) and the confounded disciples later running away from that same tomb (see Mark 16:8). In three of the occurrences, reassurance is given to relieve the fear. Luke tells of the women being frightened but immediately reassured in the presence of the angel at the tomb (see 24:5). And in Matthew, first the angel and later Jesus tell the women, "Do not be afraid" (28:5,10). Sandwiched between these reassurances in Matthew, the word conveys a sense of reverent joy (see 28:8).

Fear is accompanied by several other wonder-evoking words—*amazed* (Mark 16:5-6), *trembling, astonishment* (Mark 16:8), *perplexed* (Luke 24:4), *frightened* (Luke 24:5), *wondering* (Luke 24:12). The ease with which the same root word of *fear*—first as a noun and then as a verb—can be used so differently but without confusion in context is evident in the Matthew reference: "For fear of him the guards did shake, and became as dead men. And the angel answered and said unto the women, Fear not" (28:4-5, KJV).

Where Spiritual Formation Goes Wrong

Spiritual formation operates in a resurrection atmosphere of this "more and other" in which we have to cultivate responses of awed reverence or risk missing the very heart of what is going on. There are too many clichés and too much glibness in our language on the formation of the Christian life. Wonder permeates these resurrection stories—resurrection wonder.

The five elements of surprise here that I've gone through—the unpreparedness, the uselessness of experts, the prominence of marginal companions, the quiet out-of-the-wayness, and the fear—give a rich texture to wonder. Nothing here travels along the lines of our expectations, especially the expectations that we bring to something we consider important and life-changing. And if Jesus' resurrection is at the center of our spiritual formation—which I'm convinced it is—then this sense of wonder is a big part of what goes on. Puzzlement, astonishment, surprise. God is at work—and right here in Jesus, in you, in me.

Without wonder, we approach spiritual formation as a self-help project. We employ techniques. We analyze gifts and potentialities. We set goals. We assess progress. Spiritual formation is reduced to cosmetics.

Without wonder, the motivational energies in spiritual

formation get dominated by anxiety and guilt. Anxiety and guilt restrict; they close us in on ourselves. They isolate us with feelings of inadequacy or unworthiness; they reduce us to ourselves at our worst. Spiritual formation is distorted into moral workaholism or pious athleticism.

The Deconstruction of Wonder

Unfortunately, we do not live in a world that promotes or encourages wonder. Wonder is natural and spontaneous to all of us. When we were children, we were in a constant state of wonder. The world was new, tumbling in on us in profusion. We staggered through each day fondling, looking, tasting. Words were wondrous. Running was wondrous. Touch, taste, sound were all wonders. We lived in a world of wonders.

But gradually the sense of wonder gets squeezed out of us. There are many reasons, but mostly the lessening of wonder takes place as we develop in competence and gain mastery over ourselves and our coordination and our environment.

The workplace, when we become adults, is where this diminishing of wonder goes on most consistently and thoroughly. It's difficult to cultivate a sense of wonder in the workplace. Knowledge and competence are the key values here. We don't want any surprises. We don't want to waste time just staring at something, wondering what to make of it. We're trained and then paid to know what we're doing.

And so, for most of us, the morning after our conversion we get out of bed and go to work, having luckily escaped being hit by the Mack truck. For most of us, it is a job that excites us. It demands our best and rewards us with recognition and satisfaction. We're doing something significant that makes a difference, that makes the world better and makes people's lives better. It makes us useful and gives us money to take care of ourselves and our dependents. Work is a wonderful thing. We're involved firsthand in God's creation and among God's creatures.

A Subtle but Disastrous Shift

But then after a few weeks or months back on the job, the feelings, convictions, and ideas that clustered around our becoming Christians become background to the center stage drama of our work with its strenuous demands, energizing stimuli, and rich satisfactions.

Along the way, the primacy of God and his work gives way ever so slightly to the primacy of *our* work in God's kingdom. We begin to think of ways to use God in what we're doing. The shift is barely perceptible, for we continue to use the vocabulary of our new identity. We continue to believe the identical truths. We continue pursuing good goals. It usually takes a long time for the significance of the shift to show up. But when it does, it turns out that we have not so much been worshiping God as enlisting him as a trusted and valuable assistant.

On the job, we are dealing with what *we* know and what *we* are good at. What we know is our work. Why not ask God to help us in our work? He invited us to do it, didn't he? "Ask and you shall receive." Well, yes, he did. The problem is that taken out of the context of resurrection wonder, any prayer soon becomes an act of idolatry—reducing God to what we can use for our purposes, however noble and useful.

It rarely occurs to us to name such seemingly innocent, natural, and pious behavior as idolatry. None of us would think of placing a plastic Saint Christopher on our Pontiac dashboard to prevent accidents, installing a big-bellied Buddha in a shrine in our family room to put a break on our helter-skelter running around and pursuing illusions, or planting a Canaanite fertility Asherah grove in our backyard to promote bigger tomatoes in our garden and more babies in our nursery. But idolatry it is, all the same. It's using God instead of worshiping God. Not full-grown idolatry at first, to be sure, but the germs of idolatry that thrive in the workplace.

Slogging Through the Daily Mud

For others of us, the job to which we return the morning after our conversion—having been *un*lucky enough not to get hit by the Mack truck—is sheer drudgery. A boring, lackluster job to which we drag ourselves day after day, week after week. For a few weeks the new reality that we have in Christ displaces the burden and boredom of the workplace. Prayers murmur quietly like a mountain stream under the surface of our speech. Songs of praise reverberate in our imaginations. We see everyone and everything with fresh eyes. We are new creatures set down in a world of wonders.

And then one day we realize that the "all things new" into which we have been introduced by Christ doesn't include our workplace. We're still in the same old dead-end job in which we've been stagnating for ten or twenty or thirty years. With our new energy and sense of unique identity and purpose sparked by our conversion, we look around for a way out. We fantasize jobs in which we can wholeheartedly work, in the wonderful phrase, "to the glory of God." A few people risk everything and break out. But most of us do not. We have a mortgage to pay or children to put through college. We don't have the training or schooling necessary. Our spouse is content just as things are and doesn't want to jeopardize the security of familiarity. And so we accept the fact that we're stuck and return to slogging through the daily mud and boredom of our routine.

CHRISTIAN IDOLATRY

But what we also do is look around for ways to affirm and cultivate our new life in Christ outside our workplace. And we soon find, quite to our delight, that there is a lot to choose from. A huge religious marketplace has been set up in North America to meet the needs and fantasies of people just like us. There are conferences and gatherings custom-designed to give us the lift we need. There are books, videos, and seminars that promise to let us in on the Christian "secret" of whatever it is we feel is lacking in our life—financial security, well-behaved children, weight loss, sex, travel to holy sites, exciting worship, celebrity teachers. The people who promote these goods and services all smile a lot and are good-looking. *They* are obviously not bored.

It isn't long before we're standing in line to buy whatever is being offered. And because none of the purchases does what we had hoped for, or at least not for long, we're soon back to buy another, and then another. The process is addicting. We become consumers of packaged spiritualities.

This also is idolatry. We never think of using this term because everything we're buying or paying for is defined by the adjective *Christian*. But idolatry it is, nevertheless. It's God packaged as a product—God depersonalized and made available as a technique or a program. The Christian market in idols has never been more brisk or lucrative. The late medieval indulgences that provoked Luther's righteous wrath are small potatoes compared to what's going on in our evangelical backyard.

AN INTOLERANCE OF MYSTERY

Every Christian man or woman who gets out of bed and goes to work walks into a world in which idolatry is the major temptation for seducing him or her away from the new life of being formed-by-resurrection into the likeness of Christ.

There are endless variations and combinations on these "good" and "bad" workplaces that I've sketched. But the probabilities of idolatry are ever-present if we work— and most of us do. (The obvious exceptions are children, the elderly, the disabled, and the unemployed.) We live most days and most of the hours of those days in a world permeated with the making and purchasing of idols.

Most of us spend a lot of time at work, which means that our Christian identity is being formed much of the time under uncongenial, if not outright hostile, conditions—conditions marked by an intolerance of mystery (information and know-how are always required in the workplace). A premium is put on our competence and being in control (incompetence and out-of-control behavior will get us dismissed in short order). And personal relationships are subordinated and conformed to the nature of the work to be done.

Technology is one of the primary promoters of idolatry today. It's ironic, isn't it? Idolatry, which is associated at least in popular imagination with superstitions—the unenlightened, uneducated, primitive child mind with its myths and mumbo jumbo—now finds itself with a new lease on life with the help of technology, which is associated with no-nonsense, scientific research using the pure language of mathematics to create a world of computers that dominate the workplace and before which virtually everybody is bowing down in respectful reverence. Impersonal *things* that dominate our time and imagination offer extravagant promises of control and knowledge. But they also squeeze all sense of mystery and wonder and reverence out of our lives.

The workplace has always been a threat to spiritual formation because it is the place where we don't wonder very much. Wonder is pretty much banished on principle. In the workplace, we know that we are competent or that we are bored and inattentive. In today's culture, the threat posed by life diminished by wonder is accelerated many times over.

That is why Christian formation—formation-by-resurrection—demands endless vigilance. The workplace is the arena in which idolatry is constantly being reconfigured by putting us in a position of control and giving us things and systems that enable us to exercise our skills and carry out our strategies in the world.

Wonder, that astonished willingness to stop what we're doing, to stand still open-eyed, open-handed, ready to take in what is "more and other," is not encouraged in the workplace.

THE CULTIVATION OF RESURRECTION WONDER

Does that mean that we put spiritual formation on hold during working hours and pick it up again after-hours and on weekends? I don't think so.

For here is the striking thing: The opening scene in the resurrection of Jesus occurs in the workplace. Mary

Magdalene and the other women were on their way to work when they encountered and embraced the resurrection of Jesus. I'm prepared to contend that the primary location for spiritual formation—for formation-by-resurrection—is in the workplace.

So how do we who work for a living and spend a huge hunk of our time each week in a workplace that is unfriendly to wonder cultivate wonder, the resurrection-wonder in which spiritual formation thrives?

To those who take the Bible seriously as the text for our spiritual formation, the answer is unequivocal: Keep the Sabbath holy. This is the focal practice set down in Scripture and practiced by the church in which to cultivate wonder.

Do you realize that those first participants in the resurrection had just spent the previous day keeping Sabbath? On Friday evening, shortly after Jesus had been taken from the cross and placed in Joseph's tomb, devout Jews in Jerusalem, Nazareth, Bethlehem, Capernaum, Alexandria, Babylon, Athens, Rome—devout Jews everywhere—lit two candles and welcomed the Sabbath: "Blessed art Thou, O God, King of the universe, who has sanctified us by Thy commandments and has commanded us to kindle the Sabbath lights."

One candle was lit for the Exodus command, which

says, "Remember the Sabbath day, and keep it holy. . . . You shall not do any work. . . . For in six days the LORD made heaven and earth, the sea, and all that is in them, but rested the seventh day" (Exodus 20:8,10-11, NRSV).

The other candle was lit for the Deuteronomy command, which says, "Observe the sabbath day, to keep it holy. . . . You shall not do any work. . . . Remember that you were a servant in the land of Egypt" (Deuteronomy 5:12,14-15).

On Saturday at sundown the prayer was repeated, the candles again lit, and the final prayer, the Havdilah, closed the holy day of rest.

THE HABIT OF SABBATH-KEEPING

We don't know exactly what Mary Magdalene and the other Mary, Joanna and Salome, Peter and John, and the other unnamed followers did during those twenty-four hours of remembering and observing. But it seems unlikely that the habits of a lifetime would have been discarded. They were devout Jews, after all. The entire city was keeping Sabbath that day, and they would be too. It is unlikely, also, that they went to the synagogue. Leaders in opposition to Jesus would have been there, and they might well have felt unwelcome and even endangered.

The one thing we know they did not do is what was most pressing and what they were most motivated to do—embalm Jesus' body. And they didn't do it because they were remembering God's work of creation and their deliverance from slavery.

I'm not supposing that they talked or prayed about these things deliberately by having, let's say, a Bible study. But I am imagining that the habit of Sabbath-keeping was working subconsciously in them, providing an underlying awareness of the immensity of God at work in the world and the personalness of God at work for them. I am thinking that their Sabbath observance set them in a far larger context as reported by them in the events of Friday or by their own devastated feelings. The huge catastrophe and horror and disappointment of crucifixion were settling into a larger context of God's world-making work and soul-making salvation during those twenty-four Sabbath hours. Nothing they could do or wanted to do was important enough to take precedence over what God had done and was doing in creation and salvation as it came into focus in the Exodus and Deuteronomy commands and which had been internalized in a lifetime of Sabbath practice.

So when they set out for work the next morning, having kept the Sabbath, there was a deeply developed instinct for God, a capacity to respond in wonder to mysteries that were beyond them, to be surprised by what they did not understand and could not anticipate. Their Sabbath-keeping was a weekly housecleaning. And so they entered the workweek uncluttered with idols—all those subtle but obsessive attempts to give us a god or a routine or a program we can handle or use that get tracked into our kitchens daily from off the street. For them, Sabbath-keeping provided a certain detachment from the world's way of doing things and from their own compulsions to take things into their own hands. Keeping Sabbath—a day of studied and vowed resistance to doing anything so they could be free to see and respond to who God is and what he is doing—was basic to formation-by-resurrection in those five named women and two men narrated by our Gospel writers.

GOD IN THE WORKPLACE

The capacity to see God working in our workplace, which he most certainly is doing, and to respond in astonished wonder requires some detachment from the workplace. How do we cultivate that detachment? Keep the Sabbath.

We cannot understand the character or significance of Sabbath apart from work and the workplace. Sabbath and work are not in opposition. Sabbath and work are part of an organic whole—either one apart from the other is maimed and crippled.

The simplest way to comprehend this is to observe that God comes into view on the first page of our Scriptures as a worker. We see God working in his workplace. This is so important. Our first look at God is not as an abstraction—a higher power, eternal love, or pure being—but as a creator, making the workplace that all of us continue to work in: light to work by, the ground under our feet, the sky above us, the plants and trees that we grow, the rhythms of the year, fish and birds and animals in the food chain. As God works through the days of the week, detail after detail comes into being, and a refrain develops: "And God saw that it was good." Good, good, good . . . seven times across the six days we hear it. "And God saw that it was good." The final statement—the seventh one—is a superlative: "And behold, it was very good" (Genesis 1:31). Good work, good workplace.

And then the Sabbath. But only then. We cannot rightly understand Sabbath apart from work, nor rightly do our work apart from Sabbath. Wendell Berry makes workday and Sabbath rhythmic—one with another—in one of his Sabbath poems:

. . . workday
And Sabbath live together in one place.
Though mortal, incomplete, that harmony
Is our one possibility of peace.[3]

Sabbath is the final day in a series of days of work, all of which are declared good by God. The work context in which Sabbath is set is work emphasized by the three-time repetition of the phrases "his work which he had done" (Genesis 2:2), "all his work which he had done" (2:2), and "all his work which he had done in creation" (2:3). But the distinctive Sabbath character is conveyed by the four verbs: God *finished* his work . . . he *rested* . . . God *blessed* the Sabbath day and *hallowed* it.

These verbs all take us beyond the workplace itself. There is more to work than work—there is God: God in completion; God in repose; God blessing; and God making holy. The workplace is not the whole of life. But without a Sabbath, in which God goes beyond the workplace (but not away from it), the workplace is soon emptied of any sense of the presence of God. The work itself becomes an end in itself. It is this "end in itself" that makes an un-Sabbathed workplace a breeding ground for idols. We make idols in our workplaces when we reduce our relationships to functions that we can manage. We make idols in our workplaces when we reduce work to the dimensions of our egos and our control.

AN OPEN RECEPTIVITY TO GOD

These days, the secular world around us is giving considerable attention to Sabbath-keeping. Corporations have discovered its benefits in health, relationships, and even in productivity in the workplace. Articles and books are showing up touting the wonderful returns that come from rest, from breaking workaholic compulsions, and so forth. All this may be true. But that's not why we keep the Sabbath. We are not primarily interested in a longer life or emotional maturity or a better golf game. We're interested in God and Christ being formed in us. We're interested in spiritual formation-by-resurrection.

Sabbath is not primarily about us or how it benefits us. It is about God and how God forms us. It is not, in the first place, about what we do or don't do. It's about God completing and resting and blessing and sanctifying. These are all things that we don't know much about. They are beyond us, but they are not beyond our recognition and participation. Sabbath does, however, mean stopping and being quiet long enough to see, open-eyed with wonder—resurrection wonder. As we stand or sit in surprised and open receptivity to what is beyond us, our souls are formed by what we cannot work up or take charge of. We respond and enter into what God continues to do in the foundations and in the context of our work and workplace. Christians call this resurrection.

Jesus said, "Breakfast is ready." Not one of the disciples dared ask, "Who are you?" They knew it was the Master.

Jesus then took the bread and gave it to them. He did the same with the fish. (JOHN 21:12-13, MSG)

CHAPTER TWO

Resurrection Meals

Some time ago, my friend Brenda flew to Chicago for a visit with her daughter's family, and especially with her granddaughter, Charity. Charity is five years old—a plump, cute, highly verbal little girl. Charity's paternal grandmother had been visiting the previous week. She is a devout woman who takes her spiritual grandmothering duties very seriously, and she had just left.

The morning after Brenda's arrival, Charity came into her grandmother's bedroom at five o'clock, crawled into bed, and said, "Grandmother, let's not have any Godtalk, okay? I believe God is everywhere. Let's just get on with life."

I like Charity. I think she is on to something.

"Let's get on with life" can serve as a kind of subtext for our pursuit of spiritual formation and how easily and frequently the spiritual gets disconnected from our actual daily lives, leaving us with empty Godtalk. It's not that the Godtalk is untrue, but when it is disconnected from the ordinary behavior and conversation that make up the fabric of our lives, the truth leaks out. A phrase from Psalm 116:9—"I walk before the LORD in the land of the living"—clears the ground and gives some perspective on Charity and "let's just get on with life."

DISCONNECTING GOD AND LIFE

It's not an uncommon thing among us that a disconnection takes place between our Christian identity and God, between our friends and God, between our work and God. Then there is no more life—just Godtalk. The life leaks out, and we are left flat.

I'm interpreting Charity's five o'clock greeting to her grandmother as a diagnostic response to a way of life that somehow gets God and life disconnected and separated into two different categories. She missed something in the way her first grandmother talked about God, and she was hoping her second grandmother wouldn't also miss it. I'm guessing that what she missed was life—*the Life*. Let's get on with life.

It would be possible to interpret Charity's words quite differently from what I am proposing to do. It's possible she was saying that God is background—the background to everything—but only background. "I'm the important one. What I'm thinking and doing and wanting is what is at the center. So let's get on with what is important to me right now—living *my* way, living *my* agenda. God is a given. He doesn't need to be consulted or talked about. We are . . . I am . . . the action is right now. Let's get on with life."

From the mouth of a seventeen-year-old or a thirty-six-year-old or a fifty-two-year-old, that's probably what those words would mean. It's what many and perhaps most people mean when they make variations on the phrase, "Let's get on with life." And this is usually left unsaid: "Let's leave God out of it. Let's not complicate things with a lot of Godtalk."

But because I know Charity somewhat, I think I'm safe in interpreting her in a better light. I think she was asking for a relationship with her second grandmother in which God would not be depersonalized into Godtalk but would be a personal presence alive in their dailyness—that there would be exchanges in which God and life are organically connected.

Charity is still living in that unselfconscious, spontaneous childhood world in which everything is immediate and personal and relational. Soon enough, that relational connectedness, that personal immediacy will start coming apart for Charity. And when it does, she is going to need someone to help her out of it. Words will be turned into abstract ideas instead of working metaphors. Persons will end up being functions or roles instead of souls and living encounters. When that happens—and it most surely will, long before she herself becomes a grandmother—she is going to need someone to call her on the carpet and say, "Charity, let's not have any Godtalk, okay? I believe God is everywhere. Let's just get on with life."

WITNESSES TO LIFE IN THE PRESENCE OF DEATH

This is what I want to insist upon in our Christian identity and in our Christian growth and formation as Christ is being formed within us. Our life, our formation-by-resurrection, is bound up with maintaining this fundamental organic connection between God and life—the land of the living. We're here to give witness to where life comes from, how it develops, how we enter it. And when we notice that language or perceptions about life are becoming disconnected from the living God, degenerating or disintegrating into the dead language of Godtalk, we protest.

When Charity is thirty years old and the disconnect has happened for her, I wonder who will be there for her. A child? Quite possibly. Children are primary witnesses in these matters. Isaiah said it most succinctly: "And a little child shall lead them" (11:6). Later, Jesus famously confirmed Isaiah's insight into the key role children play in kingdom matters (see Matthew 18:1-6; Mark 10:13-16). Children are our first defense against the deadening and flattening effects of disconnecting God and life. If there is no child at hand for Charity when she's thirty, maybe her pastor will do it. Although given the track record of pastors in this regard, we shouldn't count on it. But who knows? Witnesses to the resurrection come up in any number of unlikely men and women and often in the oddest places and times. Who in the first century would ever have cast Mary Magdalene for the role?

I'm attracted by the way Charity's early-morning greeting to her sleepy grandmother leads into this wonderful psalm sentence: "I walk before the LORD in the land of the living." This life-witnessing sentence is embedded—this is what's interesting—in references to death. We are participants and witnesses to life, but we are surrounded and threatened by death. Preceding the phrase "the land of the living," Psalm 116 describes the death threats:

> The snares of death encompassed me;
> The pangs of Sheol laid hold on me;
> I suffered distress and anguish.

Then I called on the name of the LORD:
"O LORD, I beseech thee, save my *life!*" (verses
3-4, emphasis added)

The accent in the psalm is on *life*—my life, our life. Every living death-threatened person we meet on the street, with whom we work, who sits at our breakfast table or eats lunch with us, who comes to dinner, who takes his or her place in our pews . . . "save my life."

Everyone around us is alive, more or less, biologically. Biology is part of our living, but it is not the biggest part. Heart, lungs, brain, kidneys, blood, muscles—these provide only the bare-bones beginnings for living. The biggest part is God—God's truth and beauty and goodness in which we are immersed like birds flying through the air; the salvation of Jesus that splits history, both world history and our personal histories, into before and after; the presence of God in our lives by the Holy Spirit blessing and affirming us whether we're aware of it or not—and we're mostly not aware of it; the revelation of God in the Scriptures so that we know what's going on and how to get in on it.

Living, once our lungs get working and our hearts pumping, mostly has to do with God. And that's why we are Christians—to participate in and give witness to that.

LIFE IN THE LAND OF THE LIVING

The psalmist's phrase "I walk before the LORD in the land of the living" comes out of a context marked by death: "the snares of death" and "the cords of death" (NIV). There are, in fact, thirteen references to life-threatening elements in this fairly brief Psalm 116: snares of death, pangs of Sheol, distress, anguish, save my life, brought low, death, tears, stumbling, greatly afflicted, consternation, death of his saints, my bonds. That adds up to a lot of trouble. This is our context. The land of the living is dangerous country. A lot goes wrong. There is a lot of trouble brewing out there and in here. Resurrection takes place in the country of death.

The land of the living is obviously not a vacation paradise. It's more like a war zone. And that's where we Christians are stationed, along with the children, to affirm the primacy of life over death, to give a witness to the connectedness and preciousness of all life, to engage in the practice of resurrection.

We do this by gathering in congregations and regular worship before our life-giving God and our death-defeating Christ and our life-abounding Holy Spirit. We do it by reading, pondering, teaching, and preaching the Word of Life as it is revealed in our Scriptures. We do it by baptizing men, women, and children in the name of the Trinity, nurturing them into a resurrection life. We do it by eating the life of Jesus in the bread and wine of the Eucharist. We do it by visiting prisoners, feeding the hungry, clothing the naked, welcoming the stranger, healing the sick, working for justice, loving our enemies, raising our children, doing our everyday work to the glory of God.

When I go through a list like that, the first thing that strikes me—and I hope you—is that it's all pretty ordinary. It doesn't take a great deal of training or talent to do any of it. Not the training of a brain surgeon, let's say, or the talent of a concert pianist. Except for the preaching and sacraments part, children can do much of it as well or nearly as well as any of us. But—and here's the thing—all of it is life-witnessing and life-affirming work. And if the life drains out of it, there is nothing left. It's just Godtalk.

In the process of going about these life-giving, life-affirming tasks that derive from our Christian identities, we are easily and commonly distracted, diverted from life itself, from God alive. It is uncommonly difficult to stay centered and absorbed in our primary life-affirming, life-witnessing work. We continue to perform the vast array of activities in work and conversation that I've listed, and more than that. But we are also under the continual threat of death, of becoming disconnected from life and people and God and just going through the biological motions—mouthing clichés and not participating in life itself.

THE LOSS OF OUR RESURRECTION IDENTITY

This distraction and diversion is what makes for a crisis in Christian identity—a crisis current among us. Our basic connection to life is severed, and we begin borrowing our identities from therapists and entertainers, CEOs and politicians, pastors and teachers, men and women who appear to be on the frontlines and making a difference in the world.

So what I want to do is reaffirm this primary identity that we've been given by the resurrection of Jesus. This identity is nurtured and matured in our formation-by-resurrection.

It's a curious thing but not uncommon for Christians to begin well and gradually get worse. Instead of progressing like a pilgrim from strength to strength, we regress. Just think of the Christians you really admire. Aren't most of them recent converts? Isn't it exciting? Then think of the Christians that you're just bored to death with. Aren't they people who have been Christians for forty or fifty years? They are wearing out—not just in body but in everything else too. There are exceptions, of course.

We lose our vitality. We become dull. We continue to go through these life-affirming, Christ-honoring motions, but our hearts are no longer in it.

The regression is rarely dramatic. It's not sudden. We start out with life, life, life, and more life. God is primary and present in all we do. But then while we're happily and innocently going about our work, our feet get tangled up in those cords of Sheol, those ropes of death. It is so casual at first that we hardly notice. But then one cord gets attached—who knows how?—to an ankle by a double half hitch. Then there's another and another. Before we know it, we are regressing. We are hobbled. We become less. We lose the immediacy, spontaneity, and exuberance of resurrection life.

Interestingly, this often takes place at the same time we're becoming successful in the eyes of our peers, associates, employers, or congregations. But the life is leaking out. God and life have become disconnected.

Using Charity's "Let's just get on with life" and the psalmist's "I walk before the LORD in the land of the living," I want to continue to build something of a dike against some of the forces that erode our resurrection identity. I think this is the most important thing we can be doing. But American Christians are conspicuously inattentive. We have this rich, rich tradition of formation-by-resurrection—why are so few interested? I've been a pastor for forty-three years now, and I'm appalled by my brother and sister pastors who are just not interested. There are so many more exciting things to do. But this is patient, cumulative, careful, artful work that needs constant attention, and we're not giving it the attention it needs.

ORDINARY MEALS ARE FORMATIONAL

I want to try to snip some of these life-hobbling cords of Sheol off our ankles by giving attention to resurrection meals. Jesus' resurrection is twice revealed in the setting of a meal. Two of our Gospel writers—Luke and John—insist on the importance of resurrection meals. The unimaginable transcendence of resurrection is assimilated into the most routine and ordinary of actions—eating a meal. We have a long tradition among Christians, given shape and content by our Scriptures, that practices the preparing, serving, and eating of meals as formational for living the resurrection. A culture of inhospitality forebodes resurrection famine.

Luke's meal was eaten on the day of the resurrection at the end of the seven-mile walk from Jerusalem to

Emmaus (see 24:13-32). Two people, Cleopas and a friend (or, as some people think, his wife) were joined by a third person they did not recognize. The unrecognized stranger picked up a conversation with them.

The subject of the conversation was, of course, Jesus. It's probable that it was a long conversation, of which we have only a summary here. My guess is that they walked and talked for two, maybe even three, hours. I calculate that from my experience in walking with my wife, Jan. When we walk together and don't dawdle too much, we go at a pace of about twenty minutes a mile, or three miles an hour. Conversation usually slows us down to something more like two miles an hour. Jan and I usually have binoculars, and that slows us down even more. But, if Jesus joined those two within a mile or so of setting out to Emmaus, and they walked and talked together for about six miles, that comes out to roughly two or three hours. That's enough time to go into things in considerable depth.

In the Presence of Resurrection

Luke tells us that the conversation went over the details of the trial and crucifixion of Jesus, which was still very fresh in their minds. They discussed their thoughts and feelings about Jesus: the immense authority and sense of divine presence they associated with him. They described him as "a prophet, dynamic in work and word" (verse 19, MSG). They talked about the expectations that had been aroused in them. Those centuries of accumulating hopes planted by the prophets and nurtured in the prayers and study and faithful living of generation after generation of the Hebrew people had germinated in them: "We had our hopes up that he was the One, the One about to deliver Israel" (verse 21, MSG). And, of course, they mentioned the rumors that were buzzing back in Jerusalem: "Some of our women have completely confused us. Early this morning they were at the tomb and they couldn't find his body. They came back with the story that they had seen a vision of angels who said he was alive. Some of our friends went off to the tomb to check and found it empty just as the women said, but they didn't see Jesus" (verses 22-24, MSG).

Up until then, the conversation had been dominated by Cleopas and friend. Jesus started the conversation with his questions, but then he was content to listen to them talking about him. The Emmaus-bound pair had no idea that the person they were talking to was also the person they were talking about. They were in the presence of resurrection, walking "in the land of the living," and they didn't know it.

When Jesus broke in and took up his end of the conversation, he picked up the fragments of their conversation and fit them into the large and comprehensive revelation written in the Holy Scriptures. He showed them, detail by detail, how what had thrown them into bewilderment and confusion made perfect sense when seen and heard as part of what God had been doing and saying all along. Holy Scripture is an orientation in largeness and coherence. Holy Scripture rescues us from out-of-breath stutters of distracted and amnesiac journalists who think they are keeping us in touch with what is important. As the Emmaus pilgrims listened to Jesus expounding on the Scriptures that day, they realized that they weren't dealing with the latest thing but with the oldest thing. They were, as we say, "getting the picture."

What a conversation that was! Later recalling what had gone on, they said, "Didn't we feel on fire as he conversed with us on the road, as he opened up the Scriptures for us?" (verse 32, MSG).

Then they walked on into the village of Emmaus—their destination. Cleopas and friend pressed the still-unrecognized Jesus to come in and have supper with them. The three of them sat down at the supper table, and that is where it happened: "They recognized him" (verse 31). Or, as they later described to their friends back in

Jerusalem, "They recognized him when he broke the bread" (verse 35, MSG).

THAT LARGE STORY WHOSE LAST WORD IS GLORY

Put yourself at that table in the place of the unnamed man or woman—the companion of Cleopas. This is your home. You've been away for several days in Jerusalem for Passover—this great Hebrew feast of salvation, with all the energy and drama attending it. You've been doing this every year since you were a child. The place and ritual are thick with memories and stories and songs. This is your Jewish identity. This is who you are. You are God's chosen woman or God's chosen man, reaffirmed and deepened now yet again.

Then, incredibly, the holy week is suddenly and unaccountably desecrated, outrageously violated by the crucifixion of a man you knew personally and honored extravagantly. Still reeling from seeing that bloody and tormented death, you begin to hear rumors. They are flying about. There's a totally different kind of report—"a vision of angels who said he was alive" (verse 23, MSG). What could that mean? On successive days in Jerusalem, you were hurled from celebration to anguish to bewilderment. Your whole world spun out of control. Emotionally spent, you are now glad to get out of Jerusalem. It's a relief to be walking that familiar road home, away from the crowds and the violence and the rumors, glad for the time and privacy to talk everything over with Cleopas and try to make sense of it all.

Then you are joined by a stranger who takes an interest in what you are saying. He joins in the conversation and amazingly does make sense of it all. For two or three hours as you walk toward home, you listen to him take the chaos of the last few days and, like God in Genesis, speak order into the mess. You've never heard the words of Scripture spoken so personally before. You never knew that your own experiences, especially experiences as turbulent and disorienting and death dealing and inexplicable as those in the last five days, were part of that large story in which the last word is Glory (see verse 26). This man used words to create a world in which God, right in your presence, was doing everything you had read and heard about in Moses and the Prophets.

WHIPSAWED BY EMOTIONS

As you enter Emmaus, you are actually feeling calm and almost your old self. You left Jerusalem three hours ago whipsawed by emotions. And now, thanks to this stranger, you are feeling almost normal.

It's late in the day and time for supper. You've been away from home for a week, maybe over a week. There is nothing there to eat. Passing a bakery stall you buy a loaf of bread and invite the stranger in for supper. After some coaxing, he comes in. You get out a bottle of wine. The three of you sit down to a simple supper of bread and wine. Cleopas pours the wine. The stranger then makes a move that takes you aback momentarily. *He* takes up the loaf and blesses it. The guest you invited to supper becomes the host offering you supper. After blessing the bread, he breaks it and gives it to you and to Cleopas. Then, and only then, you recognize him. It's Jesus, alive. It's resurrection.

John's resurrection-meal story takes place back in Galilee at an unspecified time (see 21:1-14). This time it was a breakfast outdoors on a Galilean beach. Seven disciples got in on the meal. Five of them are named—Peter, Thomas, Nathaniel, and the Zebedee boys (James and John). Two others are unnamed. Four are missing and unaccounted for.

These are the circumstances of the Galilee resurrection breakfast. Seven disciples had recently left Jerusalem and were back in their home country of Galilee. They were there under orders from the risen Jesus himself. Matthew told us this story: Mary Magdalene and "the other Mary" were at the empty tomb on resurrection morning and were told by an angel that Jesus had risen and that they were to go tell the disciples that he would meet them in Galilee. As they were hurrying to pass on the news, Jesus himself greeted them. He told them the same thing: "Tell my brothers that they are to go to Galilee, and that I'll meet them there" (Matthew 28:10, MSG).

They did what they had been told. Jesus did meet them there on the Galilean mountains set for the meeting. There he gave them their apostolic commission. Now, for reasons we don't know, seven of the eleven are back at their old fishing grounds—the Sea of Galilee. It's not too difficult to imagine what might have been going on. Peter had organized his friends for a night of fishing. After all the intensity and drama of the last few years with Jesus, he still has fishing in his blood. We can imagine that he might well feel at loose ends at a time like this. Whatever he and his friends had previously imagined or believed about resurrection didn't prepare them for what they were now dealing with.

RECASTING RESURRECTION

Resurrection, if you believed in it, had to do with the next life. It was something that happened to you after you were dead and buried and then found yourself with God in heaven for eternity. But Jesus' resurrection took place on earth. These first witnesses and participants in Jesus' resurrection obviously weren't in heaven. They were walking the same old roads over the same old ground they had grown up on and talked and worked on, with the same old people they had grown up with.

And that resurrection had taken place in the person of Jesus, whom they had watched die on a cross. We grope for words adequate to name their response—wonder, amazement, astonishment. Despite centuries of preparation, nothing had prepared them for this.

Now it was becoming clear to them—it had been several days now, remember—that the resurrection also had to do with them and the ongoing circumstances of their lives. My feeling is that this may have been even more difficult to wrap their minds around than Jesus' resurrection itself. Jesus was radically reconfigured and redefined by resurrection. And now they were being just as radically reconfigured and redefined by resurrection. Jesus was special, of course. But the disciples' familiar concept of resurrection as life after death was now being totally recast as life "in the land of the living."

This is a radical thing. It is as radical for you and me as it was for them. This might account—at least, this is what I think—for why the seven former fishermen were back fishing that night. They were beginning to get the sense that Jesus' resurrection had everything to do with their ordinary lives. They needed practice in this reorientation, and they plunged into ordinariness—the old familiar workplace of sea and the fishing boat. I'm not imagining that this was so much a thought-out plan, the kind of thing we sometimes refer to as a "spiritual discipline." It was just simply a gut feeling for this new reality they found themselves in.

"Breakfast Is Ready"

But they were not conspicuously successful. Maybe they had lost their touch. They fished all night. "They caught nothing." (John 21:3).

As the dawn breaks, Jesus is standing on the beach. The disciples are one hundred yards out from the shore— imagine the length of a football field—and they don't recognize him. He calls to them and asks about their fishing. He learns that they haven't caught anything. He redirects them to cast their net on the other side of the boat. When they do, they come up with a net full of fish.

John, who back in Jerusalem was the first one at the empty tomb to realize what had happened, is also the first one here in Galilee. He gets it. He recognizes the stranger on shore as the resurrected Jesus and tells Peter, his earlier companion in that resurrection race to the tomb, "It's the Master!" (verse 7, MSG). Peter dives into the water and swims to shore to greet Jesus, leaving his companions to the work of rowing and dragging in the full net of fish. Don't you just love it when people with spiritual experiences leave you to clean up the dishes?

When they get to shore, they find that Jesus has already prepared a meal of fish and bread for them there on the beach. After Peter helps his companions land the fish, Jesus calls them to the meal: "Breakfast is ready" (verse 12, MSG). John and Peter have already recognized the stranger on the beach as Jesus. The five others now also recognize him. "They knew it was the Master" (verse 12, MSG). Jesus then hands around the bread and fish. It is a resurrection breakfast.

The Gospel writers are fond of telling stories of Jesus at meals. The meal was one of their favorite settings for showing Jesus as he revealed himself, talked, worked, and welcomed men and women to him.

So I'm interested in looking at these two meals that clarify and involve us in formation-by-resurrection and walking before the Lord in the land of the living—the supper at Cleopas's home in Emmaus and the breakfast on the Galilean beach.

We're Formed in the Routines

First, I observe the commonly overlooked obvious. Formation-by-resurrection does not depend on a specially prepared setting or a carefully selected time and place. The norm is the normal. There is nothing more normal and routine and everyday than eating a meal.

In our culture, we typically do it three times a day—breakfast, lunch, and dinner. We eat meals first and foremost because we have to. We need nutritional food in order to continue to function biologically. The very nature of our creation requires a regular intake of carbohydrates, proteins, fats, fiber, vitamins, and liquids.

But we also eat because it gives us pleasure. A breakfast egg sprinkled with salt and pepper and tarragon, a strip of crisply fried bacon beside it, a helping of grits and butter (my wife is from the South), and a freshly baked blueberry muffin can be a minor piece of art. Meeting a friend for lunch over a bowl of lentil soup and freshly made cornbread mingles conversation and calories in a way that brings delight to most of us.

Is there anything else we do as frequently and simply that combines necessity and pleasure so unselfconsciously, unpretentiously, and commonly as preparing and eating a meal with family or friends or guests? Our common humanity is out in the open as we eat together. We need to eat to stay alive, and at this meal we're all eating the same thing—vegetables, fruits, breads. The act of eating together has a wonderful way of obscuring—at least temporarily—self-importance. Distinctions and reputations recede to the sidelines in the act of eating a common meal.

Every culture has its hospitality traditions. All of them involve the cultivation of honest relationship, the recognition of personal dignity, the mutual pleasure that comes in acts of giving and receiving. So it is highly significant that as we attend to the ways in which the resurrected Christ comes to us and is formed in us, we come across these two resurrection meals—the Emmaus supper and the Galilean beach breakfast.

Christian practice in matters of spiritual formation goes badly astray when it attempts to construct or organize ways of spirituality apart from the ordinariness of life. And there is nothing more ordinary than a meal. Abstract principles—the mainstay of so much of what is provided for us in contemporary church culture—do not originate in the biblical revelation.

Breakfast and supper. Fish and bread. The home in Emmaus and the beach in Galilee. These provide the conditions and materials for formation-by-resurrection.

Real Bread and Actual Fish

My second observation is that both of these meals were what we might call working meals. They weren't specially prepared for the purposes of a spiritual revelation. They weren't "staged." They were a natural and integral part of daily life.

The Emmaus meal came after a long walk home from Jerusalem. Cleopas and friend (and presumably Jesus also) were just plain hungry. The meal was not, in the first place, a social or religious occasion. They were hungry after a long walk, and so they ate. The Galilee breakfast came after a long night of hard work. These seven fishermen came ashore, you can be sure, ravenous. They were grateful that the fish were already frying and the bread already made. They accepted Jesus' invitation to breakfast because they were hungry.

We have wonderful metaphors in our Scriptures that use food as a way of talking about an appetite for God: "O taste and see that the LORD is good" (Psalm 34:8); "Blessed are those who hunger and thirst for righteousness, for they shall be satisfied" (Matthew 5:6); "My soul is feasted as with marrow and fat" (Psalm 63:5); and Jesus' "I have food to eat of which you do not know" (John 4:32).

But these resurrection meals were not metaphorical. They ate real bread and actual fish. Baked bread, fried fish—food for the stomach.

There is a place for getting away from our daily lives to pray and reflect and rest. Jesus is also a model for doing this: "And in the morning, a great while before day, he rose and went out to a lonely place, and there he prayed" (Mark 1:35). But however much these practices of withdrawal are useful and necessary—very necessary—what Luke and John are both making us face with their stories is that a primary place for spiritual formation, formation-by-resurrection, is the daily meals we sit down to in the course of our daily work.

Every time we pick up a knife and fork, every time we say, "Pass the salt, please," every time we take a second helping of cauliflower, we are in a setting congenial to spiritual formation. Luke and John are telling us to take these meal times seriously. Our Sunday worship is important. The Bible studies we attend are important. The retreats we make are important. But over a lifetime, the unnoticed and unrecognized presence of the risen Christ at our meals may be more formative of the life in Christ in us.

RECEIVING AND PARTICIPATING IN THE GIFT

A third observation about these meals is that the recognition or realization of resurrection is delayed in both meals. Why did the Emmaus couple not recognize Jesus at once? They seem to have been thoroughly familiar with his words and ways. Given the circumstances in the story, it is most unlikely that this was their first meeting. They had probably listened to him frequently and talked with him. The circle of Jesus' followers was small. Jerusalem, by our standards, was a small town. What prevented them from recognizing him? And why did the seven disciples not realize that the risen Christ was again with them? This is even more puzzling than the nonrecognition on the Emmaus road because they had already seen and conversed with him after the resurrection on two separate occasions that we know of—the first on the day of resurrection, the second eight days later. At the second meeting, Thomas had even touched him (see John 20:19-28).

We don't know why. But we can observe that there is

something more to recognizing the resurrected Jesus than what we can gather from our eyesight. Participation in resurrection cannot be forced or engineered. There is something of gift involved and something of engagement.

At neither meal did the resurrection overwhelm. Recognition and confession were not forced. Jesus did not use his resurrection to bully people into worship or discipleship.

There is a venerable, but I think wrongheaded, tradition in some parts of the church of using the resurrection for strictly apologetic purposes—using it to prove the divinity of Jesus. (There is a corresponding but opposite practice in other parts of the church to deny the resurrection and thereby prove that Christian faith is a variation of basic humanism.)

There is obviously something to apologetic uses of the resurrection. Paul does it. But even Paul, for the most part, brings up the resurrection of Jesus to engage us in the *practice* of resurrection.

I'm not using the word *practice* like in practicing the piano. *Practice* is a word we say when a doctor has a practice or enters his practice. It's one of those all-encompassing words that includes everything we're doing.

The Gospel writers don't seem to have any apologetic interest—the resurrection of Jesus is not compelling as such. It doesn't force belief. It is possible to be in the presence of the resurrected Christ for hours and not know what's happening. They believed as they participated and received and engaged. The meal provides the ideal conditions for doing just that.

This Is Not Magic

Fourth, lest we attempt to acquire an exact method by which we can put the resurrection of Jesus to work on demand, we observe that the invitation to the resurrection meal in Emmaus was given by Cleopas and his friend. On the Galilean beach, the invitation was issued by Jesus himself. This means, I think, that there are no fine points to mastering matters of formation-by-resurrection. We don't need to be fussy about doing things in the right way or the right order.

Practitioners of magic and adepts in the occult insist on absolute precision in ritual and incantation. One word or gesture wrongly performed, and the whole thing disintegrates. Or worse, it backfires and does the opposite of what was intended. But there are no formulas to master in formation-by-resurrection and no principles to observe. Jesus is present, either to respond to our invitation or to issue his invitation. Sometimes it will be one and sometimes the other.

JESUS IS ALWAYS HOST

Finally, it seems to me important to note that at both the supper and the breakfast, Jesus was host. He was unexpectedly so at the supper and more conventionally so at the breakfast. A meal is a host/guest arrangement. The meal itself is usually the work of many hands, both apparent and hidden. But a host, whether explicitly or implicitly, sets the terms and conditions of the meal. The best hosts do this most inconspicuously, so it might be difficult at times for an outsider to discern the difference between the host and the guest.

The host/guest reality that is present in all meals taken in common provides extensive experience in the nature of spiritual formation. The guest at a meal is fully participating. The host doesn't eat the guest's meal, for example. But at the same time, the guest is totally dependent on the host. As guests, we are at the table in the first place because of an invitation. The food was purchased or grown, prepared, and served by the host—although as guests we may have been invited to help. And the host is going to clean up afterward.

No wonder the meal is such a frequent biblical setting for experiencing the ways of God in our lives. We're totally involved and at the same time totally not in charge. But these fused totalities can be nearly indiscernible in actual practice. "Host" is not a totalitarian role. At the table of a genial and experienced host, guests experience enormous freedom and spontaneity.

Jesus is host, always. We are never "in charge" of our spiritual formation. We don't decide the menu. We don't customize the details according to our tastes and appetites. But at the same time, we are completely present and participatory, engaged in the actual formation-by-resurrection itself.

THE DECONSTRUCTION OF MEALS

We find ourselves living in a time when the common meal—or what the philosopher Albert Borgmann calls "the culture of the table"—has been pushed to the sidelines. The machine and its metaphors dominate the way we live and think and talk about the way we live.

The common meal is probably *the* primary way by which we take care of our physical need for food and our social need for conversation and intimacy and our cultural need to carry on traditions and convey values. The meal—preparation, serving, eating, cleaning up—has always been a microcosm of the intricate realities that combine to make up even the simplest life of men, women, and children. Because it is so inclusive (anyone and everyone can be included in the meal) and because it is so comprehensive (taking in the entire range of our existence—physical, social, cultural), the meal provides an endless supply of metaphors for virtually everything we do as human beings. These metaphors nearly always suggest something deeply personal and communal—giving and receiving, knowing and being known ("taste and see that the LORD is good"), accepting and being accepted, bounty and generosity ("land flowing with milk and honey").

And always, deeply embedded in the common meal—sometimes it's invisible, and we don't see it—is the experience of sacrifice: one life given so that another may live. It may be the life of a carrot or a cucumber or a fish or a duck or a lamb or a heifer, but it's life. Eating a meal involves us in a complex, sacrificial world of giving and receiving. Life feeds life. We are not self-sufficient. We live by life, and life is given to us.

The prominence of these meals keeps us in intimate touch with our families and our traditions in which we are reared, personally available to friends and guests, morally related to the hungry, and, perhaps most of all, participants in the context and conditions in which Jesus lived his life, using the language he used.

But the centrality of the meal in our lives today is

greatly diminished. We still eat, of course, but the world of the meal has disintegrated. The exponential rise of fast-food restaurants means there is little leisure time for conversation. The vast explosion of restaurants means there is far less food preparation that takes place in the home. The invasion of the television set to a place at the head of the table at family meals virtually eliminates personal relationships and conversations. The frequency with which prepared and frozen meals are used erodes the culture of family recipes and common work. All this and more means that the meal is no longer easily accessible or natural as the setting in which to encounter the risen Christ. For most of us, the machine has replaced the meal as the dominant feature and metaphor of daily living.

But we still eat meals—all of us. So the meal remains a major opening, place, condition in which we can practice formation-by-resurrection, though we will probably need to be more deliberate and intentional about it.

THE SHAPE OF THE LITURGY

The focal practice for the meal and formation-by-resurrection is the Lord's Supper. We variously designate it Holy Communion, the Lord's Table, the Holy Eucharist. This practice has, from the beginning of our Christian way, occupied a central place in our worship. There is also a strong and continuous tradition in Christian practice of treating every meal as a kind of mini-sacrament. This tradition has a firm foundation in the biblical language that describes what Jesus did when he gathered people into his presence and ate with them.

Dom Gregory Dix, an Anglican monk in England, presented a paper in August 1941 that brought a new phrase into our language: "the shape of the liturgy." He didn't exactly discover this "shape." Other students of Scripture and worship had noticed this before. But he did something with it. He gave it some prominence. He explored all the implications. It's a stunning piece of writing, and I don't think it has ever been surpassed.

Here's what he calls to our attention. Four different times we have a sequence of four verbs to describe what Jesus does at meals.

The first time is the feeding of the five thousand (see Matthew 14:13-21). When Jesus had seated the people on the ground and got the meager elements of the meal together—five loaves and two fish, as it turned out—Matthew tells us, "*Taking* the five loaves and the two fish he looked up to heaven, and *blessed*, and *broke* and *gave* the loaves to the disciples, and the disciples gave them to the crowds" (verse 19, emphasis added).

The four verbs are took, blessed, broke, and gave.

The second story is the feeding of the four thousand—another hungry crowd that Jesus is going to feed (see Matthew 15:32-39). Again, the food at hand is inadequate—seven loaves of bread and a few fish this time. As before, after he seated the crowd, Jesus "took the seven loaves and the fish, and having given thanks he broke them and gave them to the disciples, and the disciples gave them to the crowds" (verse 36).

The identical sequence of the four actions appears: took, gave thanks, broke, and gave.

The third story is on Holy Thursday—the evening of the Last Supper (see Matthew 26:26-29). It was the evening of Passover, and Jesus had gathered his twelve disciples. And then this: "Now as they were eating, Jesus took bread, and blessed, and broke it, and gave it to the disciples" (verse 26).

So here it is again: took, blessed, broke, and gave.

Luke's Emmaus supper adds another instance: "When he was at table with them, he took the bread and blessed, and broke it, and gave it to them" (Luke 24:30).

Took, blessed, broke, gave.

Paul reports the same thing when he was writing to the Corinthian church: "For I received from the Lord what I also delivered to you, that the Lord Jesus on the night when he was betrayed took bread, and when he had given thanks, he broke it, and said, 'This is my body which is for you'" (1 Corinthians 11:23-24).

He leaves out the last verb, but he gives the bread to them. So, yet again, the four actions: took, gave thanks, broke, gave.

The Galilee breakfast reported in John 21:1-14 doesn't give the full pattern. When Jesus called the seven to breakfast, he "took the bread and gave it to them" (verse 13). This time only the first and last verbs are used: took and gave.

THE PATTERN FOR OUR LIVES

This is what Dom Gregory Dix calls "the shape of the liturgy." Early on in the Christian community, worship was defined by this fourfold Eucharistic shape, and it has continued to be the pattern ever since. But more than worship was thus defined. Our very lives "in the land of the living" take on the shape of the meal, this central and dominant resurrection meal.

Jesus takes what we bring to him—our bread, our fish, our wine, our goats, our sheep, our sins, our virtues, our work, our leisure, our strength, our weakness, our hunger, our thirst, whatever we are. At every table we sit down to we bring first of all and most of all ourselves. And Jesus takes it—He takes *us*.

Jesus blesses and gives thanks for what we bring, who we are in our bringing. He takes it to the Father by the Holy Spirit. Whatever is on the table and is around the table is lifted up in blessing and thanksgiving. He offers us up and brings us into the Godhead, into the operations of the Trinity. Jesus doesn't criticize or condemn or reject our offering. "Two fish is all you can come up with?" Can you imagine Jesus saying that to you at the table?

Jesus breaks what we bring to him. All too often we come to the table with our best manners and a pose of impenetrable self-sufficiency. We're all surface, all role—polished and poised performers in the game of life. But Jesus is after what is within, and he exposes the insides—our inadequacies. At the table we're not permitted to be self-enclosed. We're not permitted to remain self-sufficient. We are taken into the crucifixion. We dramatize it as we eat the common food. The breaking of our pride and self-approval opens us up to new life, to new action. Everything on the table represents some kind of exchange of life, some sacrifice to our host. If we come crusted over, hardened within ourselves in lies and poses, he breaks through and brings new life. "A broken and contrite heart, O God, thou wilt not despise" (Psalm 51:17).

We discover this breaking first in Jesus. Jesus was broken, his blood poured out. And now we discover it in ourselves.

Then **Jesus gives back** what we bring to him, who we are. But it is no longer what we brought. Who we are, this self that we offer to him at the Table, is changed into what God gives, what we sing of as Amazing Grace. Transformation takes place at the Table as we eat and drink the consecrated body and blood of Jesus. A resurrection meal. "Christ in me."

We initiate the practice of resurrection at the Eucharistic Table, but it doesn't end there. We continue the identical practice at every meal we sit down to. For the Christian, every meal derives from and extends the Eucharistic meal into our daily eating and drinking, tables at which the risen Lord is present as host.

All the elements of formation-by-resurrection are present every time we sit down to a meal and invoke Jesus as host. It's a wonderful thing, really, that one of the most common actions of our lives is also the setting in which the most profound transactions take place. The fusion of natural and supernatural that we witness and engage in the shape of the liturgy continues—or can continue—at your kitchen table.

"Supper's ready—come and get it."

"Please pass the bread. . . ."

"Grandmother, let's not have any Godtalk, okay? Let's just get on with life."

They didn't waste a minute. They were up and on their way back to Jerusalem. They found the Eleven and their friends gathered together, talking away: "It's really happened! The Master has been raised up—Simon saw him!" (LUKE 24:33-34, MSG)

CHAPTER THREE

Resurrection Friends

The Devil does some of his best work when he gets Christians to think of themselves as Christian laypersons. In the ordinary use of our language, the term *layperson* virtually always means not-an-expert. A layperson wouldn't dream of walking into surgery, picking up a scalpel, and removing a diseased gall bladder from an anesthetized body on the table. Nor if I were the body would I permit it!

We demand competence, expertise, and know-how in people in matters that really count. We also require confirming evidence—certifications, diplomas, badges, uniforms, and endorsements. When we are dealing with anything that matters, we want the best—which means we don't want a layperson.

But there is a problem in all of this. As information increases, there is more and more to know, far more than we can handle, and so we have to depend on others—experts—to tell us what's going on and what it means. As technology increases, machines and engines and procedures get more and more complex, far more than we can ever master, and so we have to depend on others—experts—to operate the tools and fix the machines. Every day there are more things we don't know and more things we can't do. This means we require more experts just to make it through the day, which reinforces our identities as not-experts, just laypeople.

My first car was a Model A, which I could fix. I could fix anything on that car, and I'm not particularly mechanical. But Model A's were built for people like me. Now I have a Honda, and I don't even know how to lift up the hood.

This is a perfect setup for the Devil. If I can be convinced that *layperson* designates who I am and not just what I know or can do, then I am a wide-open market for experts who are ready to tell me how to live my life and, in some cases, even live it for me. Because God is the core of who I am and what I do and there is far more to God than I can ever learn and deeper mysteries in the workings of God than I can ever figure out, I'm quite willing to employ an expert to take care of these matters for me.

And so I end up delegating the operations of my soul to the experts. I no longer deal with God myself—I'm a layperson, after all. I still, of course, engage in the usual range of God-related activities and retain a considerable vocabulary of God-referencing words and phrases to which the experts guide me. I'm quite happy to be enlisted in God-projects and often pleased to be recruited to play my part in contributing and helping the trained and certified professionals—but always with a self-deprecating awareness that pastors and professors are my superiors in these matters.

Following Jesus gives way to following Jesus-experts. It isn't long before I have acquired all the habits of a consumer in relation to God, letting someone else supply all the essential goods and services. I'm a *religious* consumer, that's true, but a consumer all the same—a soul condition deeply marred by passivity.

THE DANGER TO OUR CHRISTIAN IDENTITY

It turns out that the Devil has an easy time with many of us in these matters. Without having to invest in complex strategies to destroy our souls through meanness or gluttony or adultery and risk having it all backfire by a sudden guilt-provoked repentance, all he has to do is slip this sense of layperson into our identity as Christians. Like a parasite in our bloodstream, it develops a sense of inadequacy in dealing with God. And inadequacy is not the same thing at all as humility. This, then, ends up more often than not in not dealing with God personally, because there are so many competent people at hand to do it for us. It's not long before we are no longer following, listening, or speaking to our Savior. What happened?

Well, there is an old and blunt name for it: betrayal. Betrayal—plain and simple. And not once in the process did we ever have the slightest sense of sin. Smart Devil.

Spiritual formation requires that Christians fiercely reject any hint of docile acceptance of the layperson mentality, which has such a debilitating consequence in Christian character and the church's witness. It's absolutely crucial that we recover the essential dignity and competence of every man, woman, and child in what most concerns us— God and the company of souls of which we are a part, virtues and obedience, all personal relations, touching skin and tasting food and keeping Sabbath, signing our names, and naming our babies. However necessarily and willingly we accept layperson status in matters of car repair, orthodontic treatment, Hebrew exegesis, and computer programming, we must firmly reject it when it touches on our core Christian identity and behavior.

And so we set out, detail by detail, day by day, in the practice of resurrection. We embrace and cherish a firsthand, personal life with God and one another. We stop in open-mouthed wonder before the sheer miracle of God-created life. We sit down to meals at which we discover and rediscover Christ as host. We discern the seductions of our culture, both secular and ecclesiastical. These are the seductions that divert us from a full-bodied, whole-people responsiveness to the new life in Christ. And we recover—and this is really the subject of this chapter—our baptismal identity, personally named in the interpersonal company of God the Father, God the Son, and God the Holy Spirit.

AN UNDERGROUND STREAM

A hundred years ago, G. K. Chesterton protested against the way the specialists and experts were taking over common and essential human activities. He wrote that it wasn't so long ago that men sang around a table in chorus. Now one sings alone before a microphone for the absurd reason that he can sing better. If this kind of thing goes on, Chesterton predicted, "Only one man will laugh, because he can laugh better than the rest."[1]

This kind of thing has accelerated in our society, and it continues to infect Christian consciousness, where it is most crippling to the human condition. But we are not without Chestertonian voices calling our attention to the spiritual devastation that takes place when Christians lapse into religious consumerism and abdicate their dignity and glory as followers of Jesus. There are strong and articulate men and women—some of them reading these words right now—who are urging and guiding us to go against the polluted stream of religious professionalism that has unleashed this rampant, relentless onslaught of religious commercialism, which commodifies the spiritual life and treats the church as a free market for promoting and selling programs, techniques, and devices to the greater glory of God. I hardly think God is pleased.

The resurrection of Jesus is the action at the core of all Christian spiritual formation. My concern is to reestablish this arena of action at the center of our imaginations and set it in contrast to the prevailing psychologism, escapism, and professionalism that muddies the flowing stream from which the white-tailed deer in our souls longs to drink (see Psalm 42:1). The resurrection of Jesus is that stream. It's an underground stream that feeds springs for Christian souls. Singers and dancers say, "All my springs are in thee" (Psalm 87:7, KJV).

In chapter 1, against the psychologism that reduces spiritual formation into explanation and manipulation and control, I set simple resurrection wonder—the astonished surprise of five women and two men before the risen Jesus—and I anchored that in Sabbath-keeping.

In chapter 2, against the escapism that diverts spiritual formation into a search for the esoteric, the ecstatic, and the erotic, I set plain resurrection meals—the Emmaus supper and the Galilean beach breakfast, where the risen Christ was host—and I anchored that in the Lord's Supper.

And now, against the professionalism that takes over spiritual formation and administers the process with the pretensions of expertise, I am setting a company of ordinary friends, laypersons all, who took the first course in Christian formation-by-resurrection—and I will anchor this in holy baptism.

IN THE COMPANY OF FRIENDS

Spiritual formation not only should not be—but also cannot be—professionalized. It takes place essentially in the company of friends, of peers.

Jesus' resurrection takes place in the company of friends who know each other by name, some of whom we know by name. The resurrection is not an impersonal exhibit put on display before crowds. Resurrection is experienced in a network of personal relationships. The named people remind us that the resurrection takes place among men and women like us—puzzled, bewildered, confused, questioning, and even stubbornly doubting friends. And yes, also singing and believing and praying and obeying friends.

All this derives from the Trinity: personal relations, not impersonal formation.

Matthew provides us with the first canonical account of a company of friends being spiritually formed into the resurrection life (see 28:16-20). Two women, Mary Magdalene and "the other Mary," in Matthew's telling of the story, are met by the risen Christ on a Sunday morning and are ordered to tell the disciples. Jesus calls them "my brothers" (verse 10, MSG). He tells them to go to Galilee where he will meet them.

They do it—eleven of them (the Twelve minus Judas). They go to the mountain they had been directed to, and Jesus meets them there. But it was an oddly equivocal meeting, for "some doubted" (verse 17).

How can that be? "They worshiped," true, but "some doubted." Which ones? Wouldn't you like to know which ones? How many? Was it a few? Was it most of them? A majority? A minority? And for how long? Was it momentary? Did it continue for days afterward? Maybe through a lifetime?

Here's the thing: Jesus doesn't seem to require a unanimous vote before proceeding. He goes ahead and addresses all of them simply as a company of friends—worshipers and doubters alike. And his address is a command to continue the work he has begun in and with them, accompanied by his promise to be with them as they do it:

> "God authorized and commanded me to com-
> mission you: Go out and train everyone you
> meet, far and near, in this way of life, marking
> them by baptism in the threefold name: Father,
> Son, and Holy Spirit. Then instruct them in the
> practice of all I have commanded you. I'll be
> with you as you do this, day after day after day,
> right up to the end of the age." (verses 18-20,
> MSG)

Three verbs activate their resurrection life: train, baptize, and instruct.

That's the end of the story as Matthew tells it. Matthew isn't much on local color or emotional tones or human interest. He is clear, concise, and organized. He probably had a Palm Pilot. He's an orderly storyteller.

BURSTING WITH JOY

Luke makes up for Matthew's spare, didactic style by giving us plenty of local color (see 24:36-53). He tells us the story of the Emmaus couple back in Jerusalem on Sunday night after their resurrection meal with Jesus, reporting on "everything that happened on the road" and at supper (verse 35, MSG). While the friends are rapt in conversation, Jesus is suddenly there among them. They are shaken, frightened—they think they are seeing a ghost. But Jesus reassures them, calling their attention to the plain evidence of his flesh-and-bones presence right there. Then, as if supplying an incontrovertible proof, he asks for something to eat. They give him a "piece of leftover fish they had cooked" (verse 42, MSG), and he eats it while they watch him.

Jesus proceeds to teach them how to recognize and understand him in the large, sweeping context of the revelation of the Scriptures. He announces that he is going to send "what my Father promised to you" (verse 49, MSG), and then he leads them out to Bethany, blesses them, and leaves. The disciples return from Bethany to Jerusalem "bursting with joy" (verse 52, MSG).

These are the same eleven friends (disciples) who occupy Matthew's account. But two others—Cleopas and his Emmaus companion—are also included, making thirteen in all. We don't hear directly from any of them. But we are told that they go from resurrection nonrecognition, scared half to death and thinking they are seeing a ghost, to resurrection recognition. Isn't it interesting that having once recognized him, they don't still recognize him? They lapse. Something about this requires engagement and participation. You don't take the picture and hold the snapshot and carry it in your wallet and say he's risen.

The recognition was achieved on a dual track: First, they observed his very unghostly physical body in the taking and eating of fish. Then, as Jesus taught them, they understood how he fit and brought to completion the Holy Scriptures. What they saw and what they understood came out of the same place. Things had come together: The thirteen friends finished the day blessed and jubilant.

DEMANDING HANDS-ON PROOF

John tells essentially the same story of Jesus' Sunday evening meeting with his disciples that Luke has given us (see 20:19-23). He omits some of Luke's details but makes up for it by adding some others. The most interesting and probably significant additional detail, given our interest in spiritual formation-by-resurrection, is this: "Then he took a deep breath and breathed into them. 'Receive the Holy Spirit'" (verse 22, MSG).

But John tells us yet another story involving resurrection

friends. It takes place exactly one week after the one that Luke and John both tell. Thomas, John tells us, is not present at that first Sunday night meeting. And when told about it, he doesn't believe it. He demands what he has become famous for: hands-on proof—his finger in the nail holes in Jesus' hands and his hand stuck in the sword wound in his side. Eight days later the friends are again together, and Thomas gets what he wanted. Jesus makes his appearance and greets the gathered disciples. But then he addresses Thomas by name, submitting his hands and his side to the hands-on proof that Thomas had demanded. Thomas blurts out his poignant and enduring four-word prayer: "My Master! My God!" (verse 28, MSG). That was seven words in the Greek. Jesus accepts his confession and then pronounces a blessing on all who in the days and years and centuries ahead would come to believe without benefit of touch and sight.

JESUS' RESURRECTION INVOLVES US

Paul adds a few details to what our Gospel writers tell us by including himself in the company of the first resurrection witnesses (see 1 Corinthians 15:3-8). Paul's list begins with Peter, followed by "his closest followers"—the Twelve (verse 5, MSG). He then adds a detail that the Gospel writers don't give us. He says, "He presented himself . . . to more than five hundred of his followers all at the same time, most of them still around (although a few have since died)" (verses 5-6, MSG). Wouldn't we like to know what that was like? Where were they? In the Jewish temple? In the Galilean countryside? Did Jesus teach them? How long did the meeting last? And why didn't anyone write anything down?

"James and the rest" (verse 7, MSG) is also new information. The inclusion of James is a most gracious inclusion, for this would be Jesus' brother James who earlier would have nothing to do with him (see John 7:2-9).

Paul's last entry in the list is himself: "He finally presented himself alive to me" (verse 8, MSG). Luke's account of that resurrection appearance is provided in Acts 9:1-19 and is given again in Paul's own words in his defenses before the Jerusalem mob (see Acts 22:6-16) and before King Agrippa (see Acts 26:12-23).

Paul, after the total surprise of finding himself included in the company of friends who witnessed the resurrection of Jesus, became a vigorous and powerful preacher and teacher in the first-century church. He also became its most prolific writer. His writings provide a wealth of detail on the critical and irreplaceable place of resurrection in living the Christian faith.

In the letters Paul wrote, there are fifty-three references to the resurrection of Jesus. The resurrection of Jesus is the event that sets and keeps in motion the entire gospel enterprise. Most of these resurrection texts assert either the centrality of Jesus' resurrection or the certainty of our final resurrection from the dead, or both. But six of these resurrection citations explicitly identify our present and ongoing spiritual formation with Jesus' resurrection (see Romans 6:4; 8:11; Ephesians 2:6; Philippians 3:10; Colossians 2:12; 3:1). In other words, this is not a future resurrection but a present resurrection—which is what we're interested in right now.

Clearly, Paul's witness is that resurrection is not only a doctrinal/historical truth to be believed about Jesus, and not only a doctrinal/eschatological truth to be believed about our final destiny, but also the focus for our spiritual formation—formation-by-resurrection.

Paul thus joins the company of resurrection friends whom we have met in the Gospel accounts, friends for whom Christian spiritual formation is, essentially, the practice of resurrection.

Going over this final round of resurrection stories, we get a deepened sense that Jesus' resurrection involves us with others. It forms bonds of friendship. It initiates us into a company of men, women, and children who can no longer understand themselves as autonomous selves, independent from one another. But this company is not all alike. They don't all think the same thing. Not all of them even believe.

THERE ARE NO SPIRITUAL ELITES

My first observation in this regard is that recognizing and responding to Jesus' resurrection is not a private experience. It takes place in the company of others. We know about the two closed-room meetings in Jerusalem on successive Sundays—first with thirteen and then with eleven. Paul also cites the experience of the resurrection occurring among companies of friends—the twelve, the "more than five hundred," and "all the apostles" (1 Corinthians 15:5-7). Earlier we noted the two at the Emmaus supper, the seven on the Galilean beach, Matthew's two Marys, Mark's three women bringing embalming spices to the tomb, and Luke's four-plus women on their way to care for Jesus' body.

The two partial exceptions are the first and the last reports that have been given to us. But they are only partial, for Mary Magdalene's meeting with Jesus in the garden—the first report—was in the context of much coming and going and reporting as the resurrection news was flying about. She certainly didn't hold herself aloof as a privileged "first." And Paul's meeting with Jesus on the Damascus road—the last report—was in the company of others who heard but didn't see what was going on. The immediate consequence was Paul's submission to the company and wisdom of others. Paul, in his Corinthian letter, makes a reference to this and refuses to put himself even on a par with the resurrection witnesses, describing himself as bringing up the rear and disclaiming any position. He even calls himself an *ektroma*—an abortion, or maybe even a freak (see 1 Corinthians 15:8-9). This is the ultimate, it would seem, in self-disparagement.[2]

What emerges as significant in all of this is that first-hand participation in the resurrection of Jesus did not create a spiritual elite of experts. There were no resurrection experts, no resurrection professionals.

In this Pauline text and the four Gospel stories that have come down to us, we can detect no attempt to close ranks and exclude anyone. The "some" who "doubted" on the Galilean mountain received the same authorized apostolic commission as the others. Cautious Thomas, holding off and keeping his distance from risk or foolishness, was welcomed into the resurrection circle. Jesus' scornful, unbelieving brother James was graciously included.

Jesus' resurrection is an open door. Everyone has easy

and ready access to this company of resurrection friends, among whom there is no rank or privilege.

A PERSONAL AND RELATIONAL KIND OF KNOWING

A second observation reinforces this personal and relational aspect of life formed by the resurrection of Jesus: Twice in these stories of resurrection friends, there are references to the Trinity, the company of the Godhead.

When in Matthew's account Jesus commissions his disciples from the Galilean mountain, he orders them to make disciples everywhere in the world, "baptizing them in the name of the Father and of the Son and of the Holy Spirit" (28:19).

In John's account, on the first resurrection Sunday evening, Jesus tells his disciples, "Peace to you. Just as the Father sent me, I send you." Then he takes a deep breath and breathes on them: "Receive the Holy Spirit" (20:21-22, MSG). Father, Son, and Holy Spirit—all in virtually the same breath.

The distinctive biblical understanding of God is as Trinity. In our Scriptures, Trinity is not a formulated concept. These two texts, along with a third from Paul (2 Corinthians 13:14), are the most explicit linking of the three names—Father, Son, and Holy Spirit. But everywhere in our biblical revelation Trinity is implicit. The witness is frequent and insistent that God is inherently relational and personal. So God cannot be either received or understood apart from our being personal and relational as well. That most emphatically excludes the detached intellect as a way of knowing of God. It excludes programmatic work as a way of knowing God. It excludes the cultivation of the ecstatic and visionary as a way of knowing God. God is not an abstract idea that can be mastered, not an impersonal force that can be used, not a private experience that can be indulged.

In realizing and responding to the resurrection of Jesus, we enter the full operations of the Trinity, which is the formation of the life of Christ by the Holy Spirit in the company of friends.

So we understand our formation-by-resurrection as being unavoidably personal from both sides—from our side in the company of personal friends and from God's side in the company of the three persons of the Trinity.

THE CONGRUENCE OF ACCOUNTS

My third observation notes the congruence of the Gospel writers' stories of resurrection with Paul's six resurrection texts. Resurrection brings our lives into the operations of the gospel. Resurrection gives spiritual formation its energy and character. Here are the six texts:

- Romans 6:4: "We were buried therefore with him by baptism into death, so that as Christ was raised from the dead by the glory of the Father, we too might walk in newness of life."

- Romans 8:11: "If the Spirit of him who raised Jesus from the dead dwells in you, he who raised Christ Jesus from the dead will give life to your mortal bodies also through his Spirit which dwells in you."

- Ephesians 2:5-6: "[God] made us alive together with Christ . . . and raised us up with him, and made us sit with him in the heavenly places in Christ Jesus."

- Philippians 3:10: "That I may know him and the power of his resurrection, and may share his sufferings, becoming like him in his death."

- Colossians 2:12: "You were buried with him in baptism, in which you were also raised with him through faith in the working of God, who raised him from the dead."

- Colossians 3:1: "If then you have been raised with Christ, seek the things that are above, where Christ is, seated at the right hand of God."

Here are the elements to notice:

- "As Christ was raised . . . we too"
- "He who raised Christ . . . will give life to your mortal bodies"
- "Raised us up with him"
- "That I may know . . . the power of his resurrection"
- "You were also raised with him"
- "If then you have been raised with Christ"

All of Paul's pronouns are in the plural—we, us, you, your. The one exception—Paul's "I" in Philippians—is hardly an exception, for he is giving witness to what he is intending for them to experience. He's not setting himself apart as an expert or as a privileged example of resurrection living.

The Holy Breathing

A fourth observation: Paul's insistence that we participate in the same resurrection as Jesus is congruent with Jesus' actions and words to his assembled disciples on the evening of his resurrection when he "breathed on them, and said to them, 'Receive the Holy Spirit'" (John 20:22). "The Spirit of him who raised Jesus from the dead"— that's Paul's phrase in Romans 8:11—is the same Spirit that Jesus breathed on them. Jesus' followers live resurrection-formed lives, not by watching him or imitating him or being influenced by him, but by being raised with him. It's formation-by-resurrection.

There's an interesting echo of the Creation story in this. The word John uses for Jesus' action in breathing the Holy Spirit on them—*emphusaō*—is the same verb used in Genesis 2 for God's breathing the "breath of life" into the human form he had just made, resulting in a "living being" (verse 7).

What God did in Genesis, Jesus did with the disciples—breathing the Spirit, bringing life, bringing resurrection life. The parallelism of the two texts—Creation and Resurrection—suggests that they are similarly basic. Resurrection is no more an add-on to human life than Creation is an add-on to that Adamic lump of clay. It's life itself—the God-breathed, Jesus-breathed beginning of who we are and who we become by the Holy Spirit, the Holy Breathing.

THE DECONSTRUCTION OF FRIENDS

Formation-by-resurrection requires "the other." But this "other" is not just a warm body, an impersonal statistic, a human soul reduced to role, function, or need. *Neighbor* would be a near synonym to what we're talking about here, but I'm going to use the word *friend* to heighten the sense of the personal and the relational. It's also the term Jesus introduced in his last long conversation with his followers, anticipating the new intimacy that was about to come into being through his resurrection: "No longer do I call you servants, for the servant does not know what his master is doing; but I have called you friends" (John 15:15).

In this resurrection-created world, we find ourselves as allies and companions to friends, bound to one another not out of need or liking or usefulness but because there are common operations taking place among and within us. We are part of something larger and other than ourselves that we cannot adequately be part of by ourselves.

Friendship is not primarily liking another person. It is the common reality that we inhabit together. We don't necessarily "feel close" to a friend, but we require and value the companionship in a common life. In C. S. Lewis's sharply imagined picture, romantic lovers characteristically look into each other's eyes; friends stand side by side and look at something that is "important to them both."[3] Unlike a love affair, friendship is not exclusive; it welcomes expansion—the mix of conversation, the energy with others: "In a good Friendship each member often feels humility towards the rest. He sees that they are splendid and counts himself lucky to be among them."[4]

So there is a contemplative element among friends—appreciating uniqueness in one another, realizing the goodness that derives from a reality outside and beyond who I am as such, who you are as such.

THE COMPANY OF THE COINHERENCE

Charles Williams, a good friend of C. S. Lewis, coined the phrase (I think he coined it; he used it a lot) "company of the coinherence" to mark this relationship of men and women who find their relationship developing not out of who they are in themselves but in the resurrection-formation in which they participate in common, namely the resurrection of the incarnate (God and human) Jesus. Church, congregation, community—these are more general terms that may or may not convey the same thing. I like "the company of the coinherence."

But this kind of friendship, this kind of "company," is under fierce assault in the world we live in. And that means that one of the primary conditions for participating in the resurrection of Jesus is also under assault. *Friend* is being relentlessly deconstructed. The wreckage of deconstruction leaves the ground littered with fragments and pieces from this once rich and complex term of personal and relational understanding of ourselves and of one another. We end up patching together roles and categories by which to identify and account for ourselves and for each other. Impersonal words begin to dominate our conversation—dysfunctional, resource, consumer, problem, victim, client, asset, liability, loser, winner. The minute we start using these words to describe other people, we mount an assault on the possibilities, if not the actualities, of friendship.

This deconstruction takes place in schools where psychological testing reduces the human person to what can be measured or tested. It takes place in advertising and marketing plans that boldly use the sins of lust and greed, envy and pride as bait to sell cars and financial services, clothing and travel—strategies that reduce a person to a thing that can be manipulated. It takes place in social services that sort people into problems and resources. It takes place in churches that repackage the gospel as a commodity to meet needs or as an entertainment to relieve boredom. Every time language is used in this depersonalizing way our core identity as a company of friends is eroded.

CULTIVATED INDEPENDENCE IS DEADLY

If the assault were out in the open and explicit, it would be easier to resist and combat. But it is not open warfare; it is subtle and covert. By the sleight of hand of language and the manipulation of image, we end up doing good things in a bad way or bad things in a good way.

The intertwined cultures of autonomy and professionalism—they are two sides of the same thing—are the strongest forces in this deconstruction. A culture of autonomy sets a high value on independence and self-sufficiency. It's supposed to be a good thing not to have to ask anyone for help. It's held up as an achievement to get where we want on our own. Every automobile, every computer puts us a little more "in charge" of our lives. But at the same time, it isolates us from others. We don't need others.

But what if there are things, experiences, values, and pleasures that we can have only in the company of others—like resurrection? A studied and cultivated independence diminishes the capacity for resurrection and dulls our awareness of resurrection.

At the same time that autonomy physically separates us from personal relationships with others, a culture of professionalism separates our sense of common life with others. If we have learned to rely and depend on a professional class for our health, our automobile repairs, our legal affairs, and our religious well-being, the ordinary people with whom we live—the ones we have the most to do with (our acquaintances, our neighbors, and frequently the members of our own family)—diminish in dignity. And when we ourselves are constantly treated by the experts as either consumers or victims, we too are left without much sense of dignity.

The Practice of Resurrection

The resurrection life is a practice. It's not something we practice like practicing musical scales or practicing our golf swing. It is practice in the more inclusive sense in which we say a physician has a practice—work that defines both his or her character and workday. Physicians don't practice on sick people. They enter the practice of healing. We use the word *practice* similarly in phrases such as the practice of law, the practice of diplomacy, the practice of prayer. This is the sense in which we practice resurrection—we engage in a life that is permeated by the presence and companionship of the resurrected Jesus in the company of friends.

I'm interested in recovering this comprehensive sense of the Christian life under the conditions of our dailyness and ordinariness—our practice. It's not something that we go to retreat centers and conferences and special gatherings to practice but rather the life of resurrection that is practiced in the dailyness of home and workplace.

So I've tried to locate a few simple, focal actions that keep us in touch with these immense but easily unnoticed intersections where the risen Jesus appears and is recognized and then engages us in resurrection. You will notice that I'm using the present tense. This is happening now. This is what Jesus does. He is here, risen. The practice of resurrection is noticing and entering in and engaging.

We observed in chapter 1 that rest and leisure—the disengagement from responsibility and necessity—allows us to see the primacy of God's presence and work in all of life. In other words, we enter conditions in which we are capable of being surprised by what is other than us, other than what we do or don't do. And we are then in a place where we are capable of wonder and astonishment at what is—and who God is.

Sabbath-keeping is the sacramental act that our people-of-God ancestors have employed, under commandment, to preserve a reverent and worshiping capacity to be aware of and responsive to what is other than us, so that we are responsive to formation-by-resurrection.

And then we observed in chapter 2 that the eating of

meals is an activity in which we all engage; it enacts the sacrificial exchange between life and death, giving and receiving. That provides our access to formation-by-resurrection. We observed that Jesus' meals held a central place in the exposition of his life and that two of these meals were primary events in the recognition of resurrection.

The Eucharistic Table—the Lord's Table—then becomes the sacramental practice for Christians that maintains our resurrection focus in the dailyness of life. The Table and the Meal engage us in the sacrificial exchanges of life and death that cultivate formation-by-resurrection.

NAMING AND BEING NAMED IN HOLY BAPTISM

Now, in the practice of resurrection friends, I want to note that naming and being named is the act that sets us apart as unique image-of-God creations—souls. In the company of all other souls, it asserts the dignity of our personal identity in formation-by-resurrection.

The sacrament of holy baptism is the practice that keeps this in focus. In baptism, we are personally named in the context and in the company of the named and three-personal Trinity. As a consequence, we are irreducibly personal. Holy baptism is the sacramental act that maintains that identity and keeps it in focus as we are engaged in formation-by-resurrection.

Difficulties in the practice of this resurrection life—cultivating this life that honors the Spirit who raised up Jesus and now raises us up with Jesus—occur sooner or later, usually sooner for most of us. Some of us who have been given this new life soon want to take it over and run it more or less on our own. Others of us who are unsure of ourselves and inexperienced in such high and holy matters revert to old habits of calling in a professional and paying him or her to tell us what to do and think so we can give our full attention to the things of immediate concern. Most of us do a little of both. We have lived a long time in this culture of autonomy and professionalization. It's hard to break these old and culturally reinforced habits and assumptions.

KEEPING OUR RESURRECTION IDENTITY

So what do we do to maintain our essential identity as souls in the image of God in a company of resurrection friends? How do we sustain our unique identity as a company of resurrection friends against the isolating and professionalizing forces of our culture? The answer is very clear and quite simple: We submit to holy baptism, and then we remember our baptism. This is where we were named, and this is how we were named. This is the company in which we are named.

What we're after is an understanding and a living out of our true identity—this resurrection identity that requires living in company with men and women whom Jesus calls to follow him. Holy baptism is the focal practice of the resurrection community that once and for all tells us who we are in the company we seek as we follow Jesus.

Jesus' baptism at the Jordan was marked by the descent of the Spirit on and into him, the announcement of his intimate Trinitarian identity—"my beloved Son" (Mark 1:11)—and the launch of his public work of proclaiming the kingdom of God.

In Matthew's account, as the resurrected Jesus gives his final instructions to his disciples from the Galilean mountain for the continuation of his work to all the people all over the world, he commands them to baptize in the name of the Father, Son, and Holy Spirit.

The baptism of the first community of Christians in Jerusalem was similarly marked by the descent of the Holy Spirit among them, at which time they began to speak the language and do the work of God's kingdom in the world.

Paul fuses the resurrection stories of the four evangelists into the language of personal participation articulated in baptism. The Christian life is a Jesus-resurrection life, a life in us that is accomplished by the Holy Spirit and given focus in baptism. In this way, holy baptism becomes the focal practice for understanding and living as resurrection friends, that is, in the holy company of persons likewise defined by and included in the operations of the Holy Trinity.

Just as Jesus' birth and death come together and become resurrection, so our birth and death come together and become resurrection. Holy baptism marks and defines us in a life of formation-by-resurrection.

Holy baptism is a radical step away from our culture and a total redefinition of who we are. Every Christian tradition, with the exception of the Society of Friends, marks the resurrection life with the ritual of baptism. Given the many different and complex ways in which Christians have understood and taken their stand on nearly everything, this is a remarkable consensus. Not everyone believes the same thing about what it means or how to do it, but they all do it—marking the beginning of the new resurrection life in Christ.

Turn Around!

Two imperatives are implicit, across the board as far as I know, in the practice of baptism. Neither is difficult to understand, but it takes a lifetime of attention and discipline to be formed by them. The two words are *repent* and *follow*.

Repent is the no and *follow* is the yes of formation-by-resurrection. The two words have to be worked out in changing and various conditions through the life of the community in each personal life. We never master either command to the extent that we graduate and go on to higher things. They are basic and remain basic.

Repent is an action word. It means to change direction: "You're going the wrong way, thinking the wrong thoughts, imagining everything backward." The first thing we do in a company of resurrection friends is quit whatever we are doing. Regardless of what it is, it is almost sure to be wrong, no matter how hard we are trying and no matter how well intentioned we are. We all have been tainted by these assumptions of autonomy and professionalization. We think we're in charge or should be. We're the measure of all things. Everything depends on us. We're traveling a broad road paved with good intentions, expertly engineered, and with the latest technologies to get us where we want to go efficiently and quickly and with the least inconvenience. There are impressive experts lined up at nearly every turn to tell us how to get there even more efficiently and more quickly. It's a heavily trafficked road—noisy, polluted, with many accidents and fatalities. But it gets us where we want to go, so we put up with almost anything to get there.

Then the Gospel word comes: repent. Turn around; change your way of thinking and your way of imagining; leave the noise, the pollution, the clutter, the depersonalizing efficiency, the technology-enabled hurry, the professionally enabled nonparticipation, the community-diminishing autonomy. You are on holy ground in the company of holy people. You need to protect it from profane stomping and trampling.

We cultivate the resurrection life not by adding something to our lives but by denouncing the frenetic ego life, clearing out the cultural and religious clutter, turning our backs on what we commonly summarize as "the world, the flesh, and the Devil." Our lives are too busy and our schedules are too busy and our churches, which are supposed to be our allies in this business, are far, far too busy.

THE YES AFTER THE NO

The second command activated in holy baptism is *follow*.
Follow Jesus. Following Jesus is the yes that comes after
the no. We have renounced self-initiative for Jesus-obedi-
ence. We have renounced clamoring assertions and
replaced them with quiet listening. We watch Jesus work.
We listen to Jesus speak. We accompany Jesus into new
relationships, odd places, odd people. We pray our prayers
in Jesus' name. Keeping company with Jesus, observing
what he does, and listening to what he says develop into a
life of answering God, a life of responding to God, which
is a life of prayer. Following Jesus is not a robotic lockstep,
marching in a straight line after Jesus. The following gets
inside us, becomes internalized, gets into our muscles and
nerves. It's much more like a ramble, and it becomes
prayer.

Prayer is what develops in us after we step out of the
center and begin responding to the center, to Jesus. That
response is always physical—a following with other followers. For Jesus is going someplace with a company of people.
He is going to Jerusalem. He is going with baptized or
soon-to-be baptized followers, and he is going to the Father.
We follow Jesus by cultivating a life of prayer in Jesus'
name, finding that his Spirit is praying in us and through

us to the Father. And in our following, we develop conversations with our resurrection friends, practicing the noticing and appreciating and loving of the Trinitarian life of God-in-relationship. We are in the world of the Trinity where all is attention and adoration, sacrifice and hospitality, obedience and love.

Because we do not baptize ourselves—it is always something done to us by God in the community—the resurrection life begins and can only begin as previous to us, beyond and other than us, so that we can, for the first time, enter into and become our true God-defined selves—selves in relationship with resurrection friends. It is always done with the assent, participation, and affirmation of a company of faithful men and women who are likewise defined by holy baptism. It is at once naming, repentance, death, resurrection, and following Jesus.

In holy baptism, our lives are defined by resurrection. We know and are known by knowing and being known by the living Jesus Christ. This is where we begin. It's a beginning that invites reenactment every day of our lives. Remember your baptism, for we cannot be trusted to do anything on our own in this business. As Karl Barth insisted so strenuously, we are always beginners with God.[5]

Lord Jesus Christ, we come to you with a deep sense of gratitude, care, concern, devotion, love for you, and desire to live responsively to you. We sense that we're with friends in your company of followers—friends who share the life of resurrection and want others to get in on it, notice it, and begin participating at the center of what you're doing rather than on the periphery. We pray for strength and discernment to understand the culture we are in—the deadening effects, the seductive lures. We pray that whatever has been said in these pages can be used—some of it, at least—to sharpen what we're doing. We ask your blessing on your church—scattered and dispersed and so much of it in despair. We pray that wherever we are and whatever places we go back into—whether it's pew or pulpit—we may be part of this resurrection life, knowing that you are present and doing your work. You're not anxious about what is going to happen or whether this is going to work or not. It's worked a long, long time and will continue working. Mostly, keep us faithful, attentive, adorational, sacrificial, and personal. In the name of the Father and the Son and the Holy Spirit. Amen.

Resurrection Stories

from

The Message

RISEN FROM THE DEAD

1-4 **28** After the Sabbath, as the first light of the new week dawned, Mary Magdalene and the other Mary came to keep vigil at the tomb. Suddenly the earth reeled and rocked under their feet as God's angel came down from heaven, came right up to where they were standing. He rolled back the stone and then sat on it. Shafts of lightning blazed from him. His garments shimmered snow-white. The guards at the tomb were scared to death. They were so frightened, they couldn't move.

5-6 The angel spoke to the women: "There is nothing to fear here. I know you're looking for Jesus, the One they nailed to the cross. He is not here. He was raised, just as he said. Come and look at the place where he was placed.

7 "Now, get on your way quickly and tell his disciples, 'He is risen from the dead. He is going on ahead of you to Galilee. You will see him there.' That's the message."

8-10 The women, deep in wonder and full of joy, lost no time in leaving the tomb. They ran to tell the disciples. Then Jesus met them, stopping them in their tracks. "Good morning!" he said. They fell to their knees, embraced his feet, and worshiped him. Jesus said, "You're holding on to me for dear life! Don't be frightened like that. Go tell my brothers that they are to go to Galilee, and that I'll meet them there."

11-15 Meanwhile, the guards had scattered, but a few of them went into the city and told the high priests everything that had happened. They called a meeting of the religious leaders and came up with a plan: They took a large sum of money and gave it to the soldiers, bribing them to say, "His disciples came in the night and stole the body while we were sleeping." They assured them, "If the governor hears about your sleeping on duty, we will make sure you don't get blamed." The soldiers took the bribe and did as they were told. That story, cooked up in the Jewish High Council, is still going around.

16-17 Meanwhile, the eleven disciples were on their way to Galilee, headed for the mountain Jesus had set for their reunion. The moment they saw him they worshiped him. Some, though, held back, not sure about *worship*, about risking themselves totally.

18-20   Jesus, undeterred, went right ahead and gave his charge: "God authorized and commanded me to commission you: Go out and train everyone you meet, far and near, in this way of life, marking them by baptism in the threefold name: Father, Son, and Holy Spirit. Then instruct them in the practice of all I have commanded you. I'll be with you as you do this, day after day after day, right up to the end of the age."

Mark 16

The Resurrection

1-3 **16** When the Sabbath was over, Mary Magdalene, Mary the mother of James, and Salome bought spices so they could embalm him. Very early on Sunday morning, as the sun rose, they went to the tomb. They worried out loud to each other, "Who will roll back the stone from the tomb for us?"

4-5 Then they looked up, saw that it had been rolled back — it was a huge stone — and walked right in. They saw a young man sitting on the right side, dressed all in white. They were completely taken aback, astonished.

6-7 He said, "Don't be afraid. I know you're looking for Jesus the Nazarene, the One they nailed on the cross. He's been raised up; he's here no longer. You can see for yourselves that the place is empty. Now — on your way. Tell his disciples and Peter that he is going on ahead of you to Galilee. You'll see him there, exactly as he said."

8 They got out as fast as they could, beside themselves, their heads swimming. Stunned, they said nothing to anyone.

9-11   [After rising from the dead, Jesus appeared early
on Sunday morning to Mary Magdalene, whom he
had delivered from seven demons. She went to his former companions, now weeping and carrying on, and
told them. When they heard her report that she had
seen him alive and well, they didn't believe her.

12-13   Later he appeared, but in a different form, to two
of them out walking in the countryside. They went
back and told the rest, but they weren't believed either.

14-16   Still later, as the Eleven were eating supper, he
appeared and took them to task most severely for their
stubborn unbelief, refusing to believe those who had
seen him raised up. Then he said, "Go into the world.
Go everywhere and announce the Message of God's
good news to one and all. Whoever believes and is baptized is saved; whoever refuses to believe is damned.

17-18   "These are some of the signs that will accompany
believers: They will throw out demons in my name,
they will speak in new tongues, they will take snakes in
their hands, they will drink poison and not be hurt,
they will lay hands on the sick and make them well."

19-20   Then the Master Jesus, after briefing them, was
taken up to heaven, and he sat down beside God in
the place of honor. And the disciples went everywhere preaching, the Master working right with

them, validating the Message with indisputable evidence.]

Note: Mark 16:9-20 [the portion in brackets] is contained only in later manuscripts.

LOOKING FOR THE LIVING ONE IN A CEMETERY

1-3 24 At the crack of dawn on Sunday, the women came to the tomb carrying the burial spices they had prepared. They found the entrance stone rolled back from the tomb, so they walked in. But once inside, they couldn't find the body of the Master Jesus.

4-8 They were puzzled, wondering what to make of this. Then, out of nowhere it seemed, two men, light cascading over them, stood there. The women were awestruck and bowed down in worship. The men said, "Why are you looking for the Living One in a cemetery? He is not here, but raised up. Remember how he told you when you were still back in Galilee that he had to be handed over to sinners, be killed on a cross, and in three days rise up?" Then they remembered Jesus' words.

9-11 They left the tomb and broke the news of all this to the Eleven and the rest. Mary Magdalene, Joanna, Mary the mother of James, and the other women with them kept telling these things to the apostles, but the apostles didn't believe a word of it, thought they were making it all up.

12 But Peter jumped to his feet and ran to the tomb. He stooped to look in and saw a few grave clothes, that's all. He walked away puzzled, shaking his head.

THE ROAD TO EMMAUS

13-16 That same day two of them were walking to the village Emmaus, about seven miles out of Jerusalem. They were deep in conversation, going over all these things that had happened. In the middle of their talk and questions, Jesus came up and walked along with them. But they were not able to recognize who he was.

17-18 He asked, "What's this you're discussing so intently as you walk along?"

They just stood there, long-faced, like they had lost their best friend. Then one of them, his name was Cleopas, said, "Are you the only one in Jerusalem who hasn't heard what's happened during the last few days?"

19-24 He said, "What has happened?"

They said, "The things that happened to Jesus the Nazarene. He was a man of God, a prophet, dynamic in work and word, blessed by both God and all the people. Then our high priests and leaders betrayed him, got him sentenced to death, and crucified him. And we had our hopes up that he was the One, the One about to deliver Israel. And it is now the third day since it happened. But now some of our women have completely confused us. Early this morning they were at the tomb and couldn't find his body. They came back with the story that they had seen a vision of angels who said he was alive. Some of our friends went off to the tomb to check and found it empty just as the women said, but they didn't see Jesus."

25-27 Then he said to them, "So thick-headed! So slow-hearted! Why can't you simply believe all that the prophets said? Don't you see that these things had to happen, that the Messiah had to suffer and only then enter into his glory?" Then he started at the beginning, with the Books of Moses, and went on through all the Prophets, pointing out everything in the Scriptures that referred to him.

28-31 They came to the edge of the village where they were headed. He acted as if he were going on but they pressed him: "Stay and have supper with us. It's nearly evening; the day is done." So he went in with them. And here is what happened: He sat down at the table with them. Taking the bread, he blessed and broke and gave it to them. At that moment, open-eyed, wide-eyed, they recognized him. And then he disappeared.

32   Back and forth they talked. "Didn't we feel on fire as he conversed with us on the road, as he opened up the Scriptures for us?"

A GHOST DOESN'T HAVE MUSCLE AND BONE

33-34   They didn't waste a minute. They were up and on their way back to Jerusalem. They found the Eleven and their friends gathered together, talking away: "It's really happened! The Master has been raised up — Simon saw him!"

35   Then the two went over everything that happened on the road and how they recognized him when he broke the bread.

36-41   While they were saying all this, Jesus appeared to them and said, "Peace be with you." They thought they were seeing a ghost and were scared half to death. He continued with them, "Don't be upset, and don't let all these doubting questions take over. Look at my hands; look at my feet — it's really me. Touch me. Look me over from head to toe. A ghost doesn't have muscle and bone like this." As he said this, he showed them his hands and feet. They still couldn't believe what they were seeing. It was too much; it seemed too good to be true.

41-43 He asked, "Do you have any food here?" They gave him a piece of left-over fish they had cooked. He took it and ate it right before their eyes.

YOU'RE THE WITNESSES

44 Then he said, "Everything I told you while I was with you comes to this: All the things written about me in the Law of Moses, in the Prophets, and in the Psalms have to be fulfilled."

45-49 He went on to open their understanding of the Word of God, showing them how to read their Bibles this way. He said, "You can see now how it is written that the Messiah suffers, rises from the dead on the third day, and then a total life-change through the forgiveness of sins is proclaimed in his name to all nations — starting from here, from Jerusalem! You're the first to hear and see it. You're the witnesses. What comes next is very important: I am sending what my Father promised to you, so stay here in the city until he arrives, until you're equipped with power from on high."

50-51 He then led them out of the city over to Bethany. Raising his hands he blessed them, and while blessing them, took his leave, being carried up to heaven.

52-53 And they were on their knees, worshiping him. They returned to Jerusalem bursting with joy. They spent all their time in the Temple praising God. Yes.

RESURRECTION!

¹⁻² **20** Early in the morning on the first day of the week, while it was still dark, Mary Magdalene came to the tomb and saw that the stone was moved away from the entrance. She ran at once to Simon Peter and the other disciple, the one Jesus loved, breathlessly panting, "They took the Master from the tomb. We don't know where they've put him."

³⁻¹⁰ Peter and the other disciple left immediately for the tomb. They ran, neck and neck. The other disciple got to the tomb first, outrunning Peter. Stooping to look in, he saw the pieces of linen cloth lying there, but he didn't go in. Simon Peter arrived after him, entered the tomb, observed the linen cloths lying there, and the kerchief used to cover his head not lying with the linen cloths but separate, neatly folded by itself. Then the other disciple, the one who had gotten there first, went into the tomb, took one look at the evidence, and believed. No one yet knew from the Scripture that he had to rise from the dead. The disciples then went back home.

11-13   But Mary stood outside the tomb weeping. As she wept, she knelt to look into the tomb and saw two angels sitting there, dressed in white, one at the head, the other at the foot of where Jesus' body had been laid. They said to her, "Woman, why do you weep?"

13-14   "They took my Master," she said, "and I don't know where they put him." After she said this, she turned away and saw Jesus standing there. But she didn't recognize him.

15   Jesus spoke to her, "Woman, why do you weep? Who are you looking for?"

She, thinking that he was the gardener, said, "Mister, if you took him, tell me where you put him so I can care for him."

16   Jesus said, "Mary."

Turning to face him, she said in Hebrew, *"Rabboni!"* meaning "Teacher!"

17   Jesus said, "Don't cling to me, for I have not yet ascended to the Father. Go to my brothers and tell them, 'I ascend to my Father and your Father, my God and your God.' "

18   Mary Magdalene went, telling the news to the disciples: "I saw the Master!" And she told them everything he said to her.

To Believe

19-20   Later on that day, the disciples had gathered together, but, fearful of the Jews, had locked all the doors in the house. Jesus entered, stood among them, and said, "Peace to you." Then he showed them his hands and side.

20-21   The disciples, seeing the Master with their own eyes, were exuberant. Jesus repeated his greeting: "Peace to you. Just as the Father sent me, I send you."

22-23   Then he took a deep breath and breathed into them. "Receive the Holy Spirit," he said. "If you forgive someone's sins, they're gone for good. If you don't forgive sins, what are you going to do with them?"

24-25   But Thomas, sometimes called the Twin, one of the Twelve, was not with them when Jesus came. The other disciples told him, "We saw the Master."

But he said, "Unless I see the nail holes in his hands, put my finger in the nail holes, and stick my hand in his side, I won't believe it."

26   Eight days later, his disciples were again in the room. This time Thomas was with them. Jesus came through the locked doors, stood among them, and said, "Peace to you."

27   Then he focused his attention on Thomas. "Take

your finger and examine my hands. Take your hand and stick it in my side. Don't be unbelieving. Believe."

28   Thomas said, "My Master! My God!"

29   Jesus said, "So, you believe because you've seen with your own eyes. Even better blessings are in store for those who believe without seeing."

30-31   Jesus provided far more God-revealing signs than are written down in this book. These are written down so you will believe that Jesus is the Messiah, the Son of God, and in the act of believing, have real and eternal life in the way he personally revealed it.

FISHING

1-3   **21** After this, Jesus appeared again to the discples, this time at the Tiberias Sea (the Sea of Galilee). This is how he did it: Simon Peter, Thomas (nicknamed "Twin"), Nathanael from Cana in Galilee, the brothers Zebedee, and two other disciples were together. Simon Peter announced, "I'm going fishing."

3-4   The rest of them replied, "We're going with you." They went out and got in the boat. They caught nothing that night. When the sun came up, Jesus was standing on the beach, but they didn't recognize him.

5   Jesus spoke to them: "Good morning! Did you catch anything for breakfast?"

They answered, "No."

6   He said, "Throw the net off the right side of the boat and see what happens."

They did what he said. All of a sudden there were so many fish in it, they weren't strong enough to pull it in.

7-9   Then the disciple Jesus loved said to Peter, "It's the Master!"

When Simon Peter realized that it was the Master, he threw on some clothes, for he was stripped for work, and dove into the sea. The other disciples came in by boat for they weren't far from land, a hundred yards or so, pulling along the net full of fish. When they got out of the boat, they saw a fire laid, with fish and bread cooking on it.

10-11   Jesus said, "Bring some of the fish you've just caught." Simon Peter joined them and pulled the net to shore — 153 big fish! And even with all those fish, the net didn't rip.

12   Jesus said, "Breakfast is ready." Not one of the disciples dared ask, "Who are you?" They knew it was the Master.

13-14   Jesus then took the bread and gave it to them. He

did the same with the fish. This was now the third time Jesus had shown himself alive to the disciples since being raised from the dead.

Do You Love Me?

15   After breakfast, Jesus said to Simon Peter, "Simon, son of John, do you love me more than these?"

"Yes, Master, you know I love you."

Jesus said, "Feed my lambs."

16   He then asked a second time, "Simon, son of John, do you love me?"

"Yes, Master, you know I love you."

Jesus said, "Shepherd my sheep."

17-19   Then he said it a third time: "Simon, son of John, do you love me?"

Peter was upset that he asked for the third time, "Do you love me?" so he answered, "Master, you know everything there is to know. You've got to know that I love you."

Jesus said, "Feed my sheep. I'm telling you the very truth now: When you were young you dressed yourself and went wherever you wished, but when you get old you'll have to stretch out your hands while someone else dresses you and takes you where you don't want to go." He said this to hint at the kind of death by which Peter would glorify God. And then he commanded, "Follow me."

20-21 Turning his head, Peter noticed the disciple Jesus loved following right behind. When Peter noticed him, he asked Jesus, "Master, what's going to happen to *him*?"

22-23 Jesus said, "If I want him to live until I come again, what's that to you? You — follow me." That is how the rumor got out among the brothers that this disciple wouldn't die. But that is not what Jesus said. He simply said, "If I want him to live until I come again, what's that to you?"

24 This is the same disciple who was eyewitness to all these things and wrote them down. And we all know that his eyewitness account is reliable and accurate.

25 There are so many other things Jesus did. If they were all written down, each of them, one by one, I can't imagine a world big enough to hold such a library of books.

NOTES

Chapter 1: Resurrection Wonder

1. Raymond Brown, *The Gospel According to John, xii-xxi* (Garden City, New York: Doubleday & Company, 1970), 985.
2. Brown, 991.
3. Wendell Berry, from poem "VII," in *A Timbered Choir* (Washington, D.C.: Counterpoint Press, 1998), 12. Reprinted by permission of Counterpoint Press, a member of Perseus Books, L.L.C.

Chapter 3: Resurrection Friends

1. Thomas C. Peters, *The Christian Imagination: G. K. Chesterton on the Arts* (San Francisco: Ignatius Press, 2000), 90.
2. Gordon Fee, *The First Epistle to the Corinthians: The New International Commentary on the New Testament* (Grand Rapids, MI: Eerdmans, 1987), 733.
3. C. S. Lewis, *The Four Loves* (London: Geoffrey Bles, 1960), 97.
4. Lewis, 97.
5. Karl Barth, *The Christian Life: Church Dogmatics*, IV, 4 (Grand Rapids, MI: Eerdmans, 1981), 79–80.

ABOUT THE AUTHOR

Eugene H. Peterson is a pastor, scholar, writer, and poet. He has authored more than twenty books, including *A Long Obedience in the Same Direction*, *The Contemplative Pastor*, *Leap Over a Wall*, and the best-selling *Message* Bible. He is Professor Emeritus of Spiritual Theology at Regent College in Vancouver, B.C., Canada. Eugene founded Christ Our King Presbyterian Church in Bel Air, Maryland, where he was the pastor for twenty-nine years. He lives with his wife, Jan, in Montana. They have three children and six grandchildren.